JOURNEY WITH THE PRESIDENTS
The Official Guide Book to Presidents Park

Complete text of Presidential Signs

Compiled by
Donna E. Dunston
Laurie N. DiPadova-Stocks

Assisted by members of the
National Council of Scholars

Photography by
Everette H. Newman, III
Matthew Newman

D1565040

Williamsburg, Virginia
Presidents Park
2006

ISBN 0-9759023-0-X

Table of Contents

Preface and Acknowledgments

Welcome to *Journey with the Presidents: The Official Guide Book To Presidents Park.* As you read the guide book, which contains the content of the presidential signs at Presidents Park, you walk through our nation's great history and through the lives of the remarkable men who have led the longest surviving democratic republic in the world. We expect that everyone can see themselves in the unique traits, differences, and struggles of our Presidents.

The signs contain some information that is color-coded. The colors match the self-guided theme tours. Each theme tour has its own book of expanded information, available separately. As you look at the signs, observe these:

RELIGION — Religion has held great meaning to many Americans and presidents. Recognizing dangers to liberty posed by state religion, the framers of the Constitution guaranteed freedom of religion, clearly separating church and state.

FIRST LADIES — Some First Ladies have been more fascinating than their husbands. Who got married in the White House? Had 10 children? Which two first ladies were the mothers of presidents? How have first ladies affected our country?

PROTECTING THE NATION — The United States president is constitutionally the "Commander-in-Chief" of the nation's armed forces. Find out how presidents have led the country during times of crisis. Which presidents have been war heroes? Which have used diplomatic skills to keep us out of war?

HUMAN RIGHTS, CIVIL RIGHTS, AND SLAVERY — How people are treated must be a concern of presidents. Whose administration issued the Emancipation Proclamation? The "Trail of Tears"? The Japanese-American internment camps? School desegregation?

THE CONSTITUTION AND THE BILL OF RIGHTS — The Constitution contains the rules of government; in over 200 years, there have been only 27 formal amendments ratified. Who helped frame our original Constitution? Who was president when the income tax became legal? When women gained the right to vote?

ASSASSINATIONS AND NEAR MISSES — Find out which four presidents were assassinated and which five presidents survived attempted assassination. In all, eight presidents have died in office.

We acknowledge the following reviewers of the content of the signs: Florence Clay Bishop of Richmond, Virginia; Theodore A. DiPadova of the University of New England; David Hager of Old Dominion University; Daniel McCool of the University of Utah; James Ramage of Northern Kentucky University; Robert M. Saunders of Christopher Newport University; and Hugh G. Stocks, formerly of Gateway Community and Technical College. In addition, various presidential libraries reviewed signage pertaining to their president. We are especially grateful for those guests at Presidents Park who attended within the first 60 days of its opening. A number of them shared their thoughts about the signs and some offered suggestions. We welcome any further information that guests and readers may wish to share. Please email comments and suggestions to Donna Dunston at ddunston@presidentspark.org.

Donna Dunston
Director of Finance and Administration
Presidents Park

Laurie DiPadova-Stocks, Ph.D.
Dean, Hauptmann School for Public Affairs
Park University

The Presidency

The Presidency of the United States of America is unique in the history of the world. Presidents have power like that of ancient kings, yet they are dependent on the nation's citizens to elect them and to re-elect them into office. Through those votes, the people control the most powerful office on earth.

At great personal risk, our nation's founders declared independence from Great Britain, fought a war with the most powerful empire on earth at the time, and lived for eleven years with a makeshift government created to run the war. Realizing that this government was not working, they wrote our Constitution, creating a government responsive to the people and with powers balanced among the Congress, the Supreme Court, and the President.

Presidents have great power; they have purchased land equal to a third of our nation, initiated and ended wars, and pardoned people's crimes. Presidents are also criticized and opposed. Two have been impeached, and one has resigned. Many have lost their bids for re-election. But no matter how a president's term of office concludes, at the end there is always a peaceful transfer of power to the new president.

We invite you to walk among these Presidents and become acquainted with them as individuals, each coming from a different background to carve his own unique approach to the Presidency. Each President has endeavored to carry out the duties of this office to the best of his ability. Through triumphs and blunders, good judgment and bad, for over 200 years, our democracy has prevailed because of the wisdom and vision of those who created the Constitution of the United States and the Presidency.

Everette H. Newman, III
President
Presidents Park

George Washington

1st President • April 30, 1789 - March 3, 1797

The Father of His Country

BIRTHDATE: February 22, 1732
BIRTHPLACE: Westmoreland County, Virginia
PHYSICAL DESCRIPTION: 6 ft. 2 in., 175 lbs.; wore size 13 shoe
EDUCATION: Tutored at home; trained to be a surveyor
RELIGION: Episcopalian
FIRST LADY: Martha Dandridge Custis Washington
CHILDREN: John Parke Custis (adopted), Martha Parke Custis (adopted)
MILITARY SERVICE: Served in Virginia militia; General and Commander-in-chief of the Continental Army
POLITICAL PARTY: Considered them to be factions promoting own interest. Believed himself to be unselfish defender of the common good. Sided with Alexander Hamilton and the Federalist Party on the domestic program.
BEFORE THE PRESIDENCY: Member, House of Burgesses; Delegate to Continental Congress; President, Constitutional Convention
VICE PRESIDENT: John Adams
SALARY: $25,000/year - Refused by Washington
DIED: December 14, 1799, at Mount Vernon, Virginia
BURIED: Family Vault, Mount Vernon, Virginia

ACCOMPLISHMENTS AND EVENTS

★ Signed into law bills creating or providing for the basics of the new government, such as: oaths of allegiance to be sworn by federal and state officials, establishment of cabinet positions of Department of State, War, and the Treasury, and Office of Postmaster General.

★ Tried to create regional balance in his appointments to his cabinet and the Supreme Court.

★ As President of the Constitutional Convention, he was the first to sign the Constitution.

★ CONSTITUTIONAL AMENDMENTS RATIFIED: The first 11 amendments, including the Bill of Rights.

★ Oversaw establishment of the National Bank.

★ Whiskey Rebellion: Insisting that Americans obey the law and respect federal institutions, he crushed western farmers who resisted paying federal excise tax.

★ Foreign Policy: Normalized relations with Spain by establishing the boundary between the U.S. and Spanish Florida at the thirty-first parallel, granting U.S. vessels free access to the Mississippi River and the port of New Orleans.

★ Despite France's vital role in America's success in breaking with England, he repudiated treaty with France when the French Revolution spread into a general European War. Established principle that it is contrary to American interests to become involved in big power conflicts in Europe; this principle held until World War I.

★ ADMITTED TO THE UNION: Vermont, Kentucky, Tennessee

INTERESTING FACTS AND QUOTES

✦ Only president elected unanimously by the electoral college.

✦ Only president inaugurated in two cities: New York and Philadelphia.

✦ Served as chancellor of the College of William and Mary.

✦ Before age 16, he had copied 110 maxims of etiquette in his schoolbook, including: "Sleep not when others speak; sit not when others stand; speak not when you should hold your peace; walk not when others stop."

- ✦ **Martha Washington, assuring their privacy after her husband died, burned all their letters.**
- ✦ Could have been re-elected to a third term, but resigned after two terms, establishing the precedent of presidential service for no more than two terms.
- ✦ Provided for freeing of his slaves upon his death; did not speak out against slavery but wrote in a letter, "There is not a man living who wishes more sincerely than I do to see a plan adopted for the abolition of it [slavery]."
- ✦ Many places are named after Washington, including the nation's capital, the state, 31 counties, and 17 communities.
- ✦ "As the sword was the last resort for the preservation of our liberties, so it ought to be the first to be laid aside when those liberties are firmly established."
- ✦ "Few men have virtue enough to withstand the highest bidder."
- ✦ "I hope I shall possess firmness and virtue enough to maintain what I consider the most enviable of all titles, the character of an honest man."

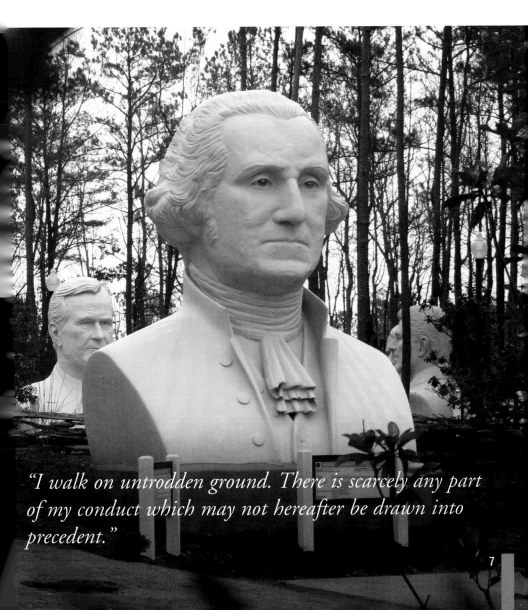

"I walk on untrodden ground. There is scarcely any part of my conduct which may not hereafter be drawn into precedent."

"No man who ever held the office of president would congratulate a friend on obtaining it."

John Adams

2nd President • March 4, 1797 - March 3, 1801

BIRTHDATE: October 30, 1735
BIRTHPLACE: Braintree, Massachusetts
PHYSICAL DESCRIPTION: 5 ft. 6 in.
EDUCATION: Harvard College
RELIGION: Congregational
FIRST LADY: Abigail Smith Adams
CHILDREN: Abigail Amelia, John Quincy, Susanna, Charles, Thomas Boylston
MILITARY SERVICE: None
POLITICAL PARTY: Federalist
VICE PRESIDENT: Thomas Jefferson
SALARY: $25,000/year
NICKNAME: Duke of Braintree, His Rotundity
DIED: July 4, 1826, Braintree, Massachusetts
BURIED: United First Parish Church, Quincy, Massachusetts

ACCOMPLISHMENTS AND EVENTS

★ Author, Massachusetts State Constitution, establishing "a government of laws and not of men" and the oldest written constitution still in operation in the world.

★ Served on committee that wrote the Declaration of Independence and led debate for its passage.

★ Helped draw up peace treaty with England after the Revolutionary War.

★ Signed the *Alien* and *Sedition Acts*, which severely limited freedom of expression by those who disagreed with government policies.

★ Pardoned John Fries, sentenced to be hanged for leading rebellion resisting tax collection.

★ To influence the next administration, he spent final hours in office appointing judges and court officials; Jefferson refused to honor these appointments.

★ BEFORE THE PRESIDENCY: Lawyer; Member, Continental Congress; Diplomat to Europe; Vice President of the United States

INTERESTING FACTS AND QUOTES

✦ First president whose son became president.

✦ First Lady Abigail Adams, first wife and mother of a president, advised her husband on policy matters; she advocated for women's rights and the abolition of slavery.

✦ Exchanged over 1,100 letters with Abigail from 1762 until 1801. These national treasures provide vital insight into the emerging American democracy, as well as into one of the most celebrated marriages in history.

✦ As an attorney, successfully defended British soldiers against murder charges which grew out of the Boston Massacre.

✦ Political adversary of Thomas Jefferson; later in life they became close friends. Both died on July 4th of 1826, 50 years to the day after adoption of the Declaration of Independence. Among Adams' last words were: "Thomas Jefferson survives."

Thomas Jefferson

3rd President • March 4, 1801 - March 3, 1809
Negotiated the Greatest Real Estate Deal in History

BIRTHDATE: April 13, 1743
BIRTHPLACE: Shadwell, Virginia
HEIGHT: 6 ft. 2 1/2 in.
EDUCATION: College of William and Mary
RELIGION: No formal affiliation
FIRST LADY: Martha Skelton Jefferson (deceased prior to his taking office). His married daughters, along with Dolley Madison (wife of Secretary of State James Madison), served as Presidential hostesses when needed.
CHILDREN: Martha, Jane, infant son, Mary, Lucy, Lucy; only Martha and Mary lived to reach adulthood
MILITARY SERVICE: None
BEFORE THE PRESIDENCY: Member, House of Burgesses; Continental Congress; Virginia House of Delegates; Governor of Virginia; Minister to France; Secretary of State; Vice President of the United States
POLITICAL PARTY: Jeffersonian Republican, nationalists who favored in principle a limited federal government
VICE PRESIDENT: First term - Aaron Burr
　　　　　　　　　Second term - George Clinton
SALARY: $25,000/year
NICKNAME: Man of the People, Sage of Monticello
DIED: July 4, 1826, at Monticello, Virginia, approximately five hours before John Adams died. Jefferson was 83.
BURIED: Monticello Estate, Charlottesville, Virginia

ACCOMPLISHMENTS AND EVENTS

★ Drafted the Virginia Statute of Religious Freedom, asserting that "no man shall be compelled to frequent or support any religious worship. . ." Held as the foundation for the establishment of religious freedom in the United States.

★ Responsible for the greatest real estate deal in history: the vast Louisiana Purchase of 827,987 square miles between the Mississippi River and the Rocky Mountains for $15 million, or 3 cents per acre, doubling the size of the United States.

★ Authorized the Lewis and Clark expedition to explore the land obtained in the Louisiana Purchase.

★ Invented many items such as the swivel chair and an improved letter-copying machine.

★ Signed Abolition of the Slave Trade bill in 1807, banning the importation of slaves effective January 1, 1808.

★ Established the precedent of Executive Privilege, declining a subpoena to testify at Burr's treason trial and to bring certain papers bearing on the case to court.

★ Foreign Policy: Agreed with George Washington about the need to avoid European wars. Imposed an embargo in 1807-08 in an attempt to pressure England and France into respecting American rights on the high seas.

★ CONSTITUITONAL AMENDMENT RATIFIED: 12th Amendment, specifying that electors in the electoral college vote separately for president and vice president.

★ ADMITTED TO THE UNION: Ohio

INTERESTING FACTS AND QUOTES

✦ Introduced spaghetti and ice cream to this country.

✦ **Martha died nearly two decades before he became president. He promised her, on her deathbed, that he would never remarry. He lived for another 47 years and never did.**

✦ Known as the best legal mind in the nation during his lifetime.

✦ Argued for equality, yet would not free his own slaves.

✦ **Considered religion a personal matter; favored absolute separation of church and state.**

✦ Dismayed that the Constitution had omitted a Bill of Rights, he wrote: "A bill of rights is what the people are entitled to against every government on earth."

✦ "If you expect a people to be ignorant and free, then you expect something that never was nor never will be."

✦ "The man who reads nothing at all is better off than the man who reads nothing but newspapers."

✦ He wrote his own epitaph: "Here was buried Thomas Jefferson, author of the Declaration of Independence, Virginia Statute for Religious Freedom, and the Father of the University of Virginia." Did not include his service as President of the United States or Governor of Virginia.

✦ A political adversary of John Adams, they later became close friends. Both died on July 4th of 1826, 50 years to the day after the adoption of the Declaration of Independence.

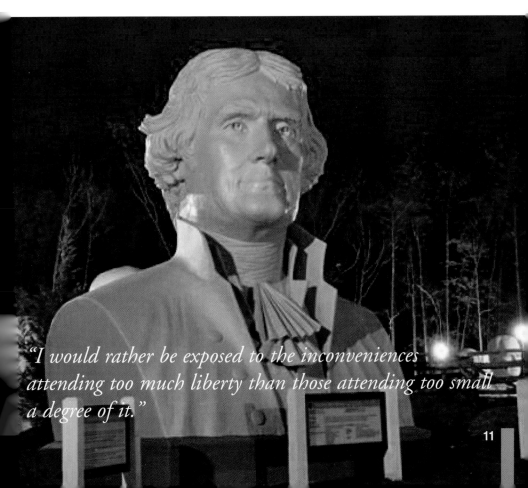

"I would rather be exposed to the inconveniences attending too much liberty than those attending too small a degree of it."

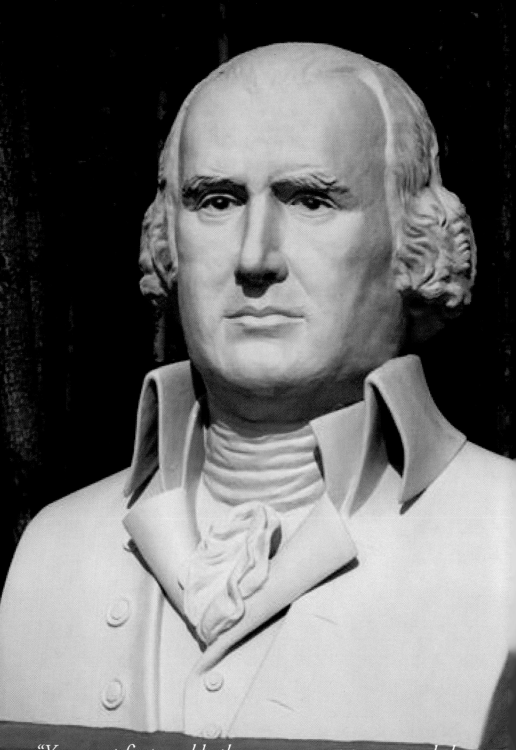

"*You must first enable the government to controul the governed; and in the next place, oblige it to controul itself.*"

James Madison

4th President • March 4, 1809 - March 4, 1817

BIRTHDATE: March 16, 1751
BIRTHPLACE: Port Conway, Virginia
PHYSICAL DESCRIPTION: 5 ft. 4 in., 100 lbs.
EDUCATION: College of New Jersey (now Princeton University)
RELIGION: Episcopalian
FIRST LADY: Dorothy (Dolley) Todd Madison
CHILDREN: None
MILITARY SERVICE: Colonel in Virginia's Orange County Militia
POLITICAL PARTY: Jeffersonian-Republican
VICE PRESIDENT: First term - George Clinton
　　　　　　　　Second term - Elbridge Gerry
SALARY: $25,000/year
NICKNAME: Father of the Constitution
DIED: June 28, 1836, Montpelier in Virginia
BURIED: Montpelier Estate, Virginia

ACCOMPLISHMENTS AND EVENTS

★ Helped frame the Bill of Rights.

★ A founder of the Jeffersonian-Republican Party.

★ Authored the *Federalist Papers* with Alexander Hamilton and John Jay.

★ Known as the Father of the Constitution, he created the Virginia Plan for government, which became the foundation of the U.S. Constitution.

★ Central concept of government was the "separation of powers," a system of checks and balances which pervades the U.S. Constitution.

★ U.S. declared War of 1812, which officially ended economic dependence on Great Britain.

★ ADMITTED TO THE UNION: Louisiana, Indiana

★ BEFORE THE PRESIDENCY: Lawyer; Delegate, Virginia Convention; Member, Virginia House of Delegates; Continental Congress; Delegate to Annapolis Convention; Member, U.S. House of Representatives; Secretary of State

INTERESTING FACTS AND QUOTES

✦ Our shortest president, he was barely 5 ft. 4 inches tall and weighed approximately 100 lbs. His hat size was 7 1/4.

✦ Dolley Madison, known for her vivacious and outgoing nature, held parties for the wives of members of the president's cabinet.

✦ Both of his vice presidents died in office.

✦ "If men were angels, no government would be necessary."

✦ "The essence of government is power; and power, lodged as it must be in human hands, will ever be liable to abuse."

✦ "Knowledge will forever govern ignorance, and a people who mean to be their own governors must arm themselves with the power which knowledge gives."

James Monroe

5th President • March 5, 1817 - March 3, 1825

BIRTHDATE: April 28, 1758
BIRTHPLACE: Westmoreland County, Virginia
PHYSICAL DESCRIPTION: Slightly over 6 ft.
EDUCATION: College of William and Mary
RELIGION: Episcopalian
FIRST LADY: Elizabeth Kortright Monroe
CHILDREN: Eliza, James, Maria
MILITARY SERVICE: Served in Continental Army; military commissioner of Virginia
POLITICAL PARTY: Jeffersonian-Republican
VICE PRESIDENT: Daniel D. Tompkins
SALARY: $25,000/year
NICKNAME: Last of the Cocked Hats
DIED: July 4, 1831, in New York City
BURIED: Hollywood Cemetery, Richmond, Virginia

ACCOMPLISHMENTS AND EVENTS

★ Ordered General Andrew Jackson to deal with Seminole Indians and fugitive slaves raiding settlements in Georgia.

★ Helped found the American Colonization Society, which transported freed slaves to the new African country of Liberia.

★ Framed the Missouri Compromise, admitting Missouri as a slave state and Maine as a free state.

★ Established the Monroe Doctrine, which closed America to colonization by foreign nations.

★ Congress fixed the number of stripes on the American flag to 13 to honor the original colonies.

★ ADMITTED TO THE UNION: Mississippi, Illinois, Alabama, Maine, Missouri

★ BEFORE THE PRESIDENCY: Lawyer; Virginia Assembly; Continental Congress; Member, U.S. Senate; Minister to France and Great Britain; Governor of Virginia; Special Envoy to Paris (to negotiate the Louisiana Purchase); Secretary of State; Secretary of War

INTERESTING FACTS AND QUOTES

✦ Believed to be the person in the boat holding the flag in the famous painting of George Washington crossing the Delaware.

✦ Elizabeth Monroe had the presidential residence painted white; thus it is called the White House.

✦ In election for his second term, Monroe won all the electoral votes except one.

✦ Opposed Virginia's ratification of the Constitution because of concerns about the concentration of power in the national government.

✦ "Let us by all wise and constitutional measures promote intelligence among the people as the best means of preserving our liberties."

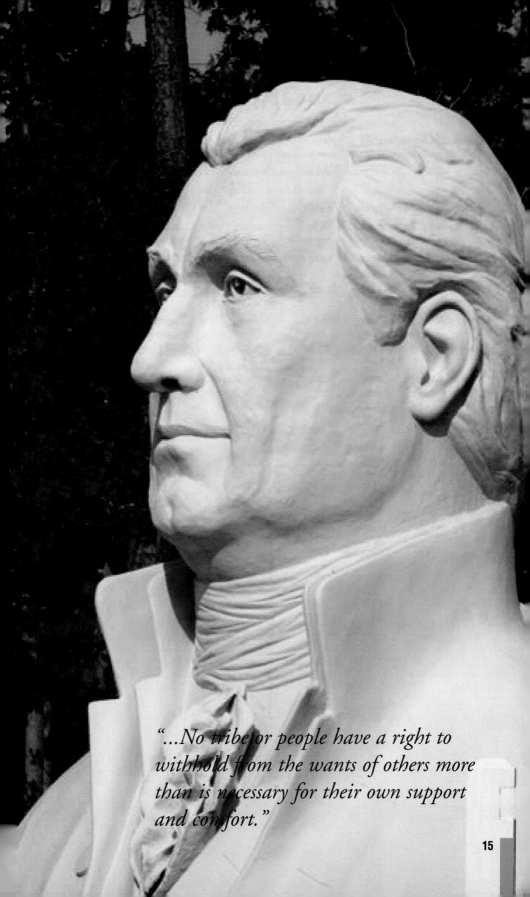

"...No tribe or people have a right to withhold from the wants of others more than is necessary for their own support and comfort."

15

"You will never know how much it cost my generation to secure your freedom. I hope you will make good use of it."

John Quincy Adams

6th President • March 4, 1825 - March 3, 1829

BIRTHDATE: July 11, 1767
BIRTHPLACE: Braintree (later Quincy), Massachusetts
PHYSICAL DESCRIPTION: 5 ft. 7 in., 175 lbs.
EDUCATION: Harvard College
RELIGION: Congregational
FIRST LADY: Louisa Catherine Johnson Adams
CHILDREN: George Washington, John, Charles Francis, Louisa Catherine
MILITARY SERVICE: None
POLITICAL PARTY: Jeffersonian-Republican
VICE PRESIDENT: John C. Calhoun
SALARY: $25,000/year
NICKNAME: Old Man Eloquent
DIED: February 23, 1848, in Washington, D.C.
BURIED: United First Parish Church, Quincy, Massachusetts

ACCOMPLISHMENTS AND EVENTS

★ Established the Panama Congress to foster Pan-American cooperation.

★ Placed a high tariff on imported manufactured goods to protect domestic industry.

★ Financed scientific expeditions.

★ Only president to serve in the House of Representatives after holding office. Agreed to run from his district on two conditions: that he would never solicit votes and that he would follow his conscience.

★ In the House, opposed slavery and championed freedom of speech. Suffered a stroke on the floor of the House.

★ BEFORE THE PRESIDENCY: Lawyer; Minister to Great Britain, the Netherlands, Russia, and Prussia; Massachusetts State Senator; Member, U.S. Senate; Member, U.S. House of Representatives; Secretary of State

INTERESTING FACTS AND QUOTES

✦ Son of a former president.

✦ Studied in the Netherlands at age 11, went on a diplomatic mission to Russia as a language interpreter at age 14 and negotiated a treaty with Sweden at age 15. Fluent in Latin, Greek, French, Dutch and Spanish.

✦ Louisa Adams, the only first lady born in another country, married John when he came to England as an emissary.

✦ Defended the mutineers on the *Amistad* slave ship before the U.S. Supreme Court; his brief became a hallmark of the Abolitionist arguments.

✦ Swam in the Potomac River every day and was cornered into giving an interview to a female reporter.

✦ First president to be photographed.

✦ He had a pet alligator.

Andrew Jackson

7th President • March 4, 1829 - March 3, 1837
First People's President

BIRTHDATE: March 15, 1767
BIRTHPLACE: Waxhaw settlement, South Carolina
PHYSICAL DESCRIPTION: 6 ft. 1 in., 140 lbs.
EDUCATION: Attended schools conducted by local educators for 5 years
RELIGION: Presbyterian
FIRST LADY: Rachel Donelson Robards Jackson
CHILDREN: Adopted one of his wife's nephews as an infant in 1809 and named him Andrew Jackson, Jr.
MILITARY SERVICE: Distinguished military career from the Revolutionary War to rank of general in the War of 1812, where he commanded U.S. forces in the Battle of New Orleans and in the First Seminole War
POLITICAL PARTY: Democratic-Republican for first term; second term as Democratic, because Republican was dropped from the name of the party
BEFORE THE PRESIDENCY: Military service; lawyer; public prosecutor; storekeeper; farmer; Member, U.S. House of Representatives; Member, U.S. Senate; Justice of Tennessee Superior Court
VICE PRESIDENT: First term - John C. Calhoun
Second term - Martin Van Buren
SALARY: $25,000/year
NICKNAME: Old Hickory
DIED: June 8, 1845, at his estate, The Hermitage, in Nashville, Tennessee
BURIED: The Hermitage, Nashville, Tennessee

ACCOMPLISHMENTS AND EVENTS

★ The first "common man" and westerner to become president; the only president to have an era of history named after him: The Jacksonian Age.

★ Staffed government vacancies with his supporters and members of his party. Known as a supporter of the "spoils system."

★ Established the precedent that the president can fire members of the cabinet for policy differences, expanding presidential power.

★ Opposed the Bank of the United States as a tool of business interests.

★ Signed higher tariffs and advocated strong federal control over states' rights.

★ Signed the Indian Removal Act of 1830 to sell land belonging to the Cherokee Indians in the state of Georgia. The Cherokees called their expulsion from their land as their "trail of tears."

★ Defied the U.S. Supreme Court which had ruled in favor of the Cherokees in affirming their rights. Jackson ordered them removed anyway.

★ ADMITTED TO THE UNION: Arkansas, Michigan

★ ASSASSINATION ATTEMPT: In 1835, while Jackson was leaving the Capitol Building, Richard Lawrence fired a gun at the president at close range. When it failed, Lawrence fired a second gun, which also failed. The assassin was found not guilty by reason of insanity and confined to a mental institution. The two handguns were found to be in working order. The odds of both guns misfiring were 1 in 125,000.

INTERESTING FACTS AND QUOTES

✦ First president born in a log cabin.

✦ Only president to have been a prisoner of war; survived smallpox as a prisoner during the Revolutionary War.

✦ Came into office as a military hero from victories as a general in the War of 1812, at the Battle of New Orleans, and in the First Seminole War.

✦ Rachel Jackson was buried on Christmas Eve of 1828 just before her husband's inauguration, her untimely death attributed to political attacks over their marriage.

✦ Duel with Charles Dickinson, May 30, 1806 - Jackson challenged Dickinson, one of the best pistol shots in the U.S., to a duel. They faced off at 8 paces and Dickinson fired the first shot, shooting Jackson near his heart. Jackson remained standing, clutching his chest, and fired at Dickinson. The gun misfired the first time, but he fired again. The bullet struck Dickinson, killing him.

✦ When inaugurated he had a saber slash down his forehead and two bullets in his body. The one closest to his heart came from fighting a duel, the other one was removed from his shoulder after he took office.

✦ First president who opened the White House for public receptions.

✦ First president to ride on a railroad train (1833).

✦ Used his Constitutional veto power more often than all his predecessors combined.

✦ "One man with courage makes a majority."

✦ "It is to be regretted that the rich and powerful too often bend the acts of government to their own selfish purposes."

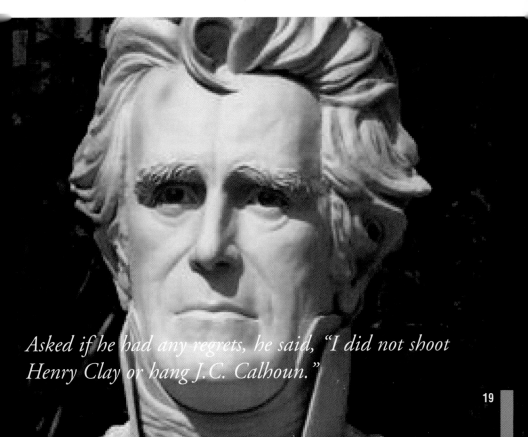

Asked if he had any regrets, he said, "I did not shoot Henry Clay or hang J.C. Calhoun."

"*There is a power in public opinion in this country...which will not tolerate an incompetent or unworthy man to hold in his weak or wicked hands the lives and fortunes of his fellow citizens.*"

Martin Van Buren

8th President • March 4, 1837 - March 3, 1841

BIRTHDATE: December 5, 1782
BIRTHPLACE: Kinderhook, New York
PHYSICAL DESCRIPTION: A bit under 5 ft. 6 in.
EDUCATION: Kinderhook Academy
RELIGION: Dutch Reformed
FIRST LADY: Hannah Hoes Van Buren
CHILDREN: Abraham, John, Martin, Winfield, Smith
MILITARY SERVICE: None
POLITICAL PARTY: Democratic
VICE PRESIDENT: Richard M. Johnson
SALARY: $25,000/year
NICKNAME: Little Magician, The Red Fox, OK, Old Kinderhook
DIED: July 24, 1862, Lindenwald Estate in Kinderhook, New York
BURIED: Kinderhook Cemetery, Kinderhook, New York

ACCOMPLISHMENTS AND EVENTS

★ Responding to the economic panic of 1837, where 900 banks collapsed and unemployed citizens held food riots, Van Buren enacted a plan for independent federal treasury which protected federal funds.

★ Rather than go to war over the border between Maine and the province of New Brunswick, he sent General Winfield Scott to arrange a truce.

★ Engaged in the Second Seminole War in Florida, drawing criticism for continuing Jackson's Indian policy of forced removal.

★ Constitutional restrictions on federal powers prevented him from intervening when the Governor of Missouri issued an extermination order against Mormons.

★ BEFORE THE PRESIDENCY: Lawyer; Member, New York State Senate; Member, U.S. Senate; Governor of New York; Secretary of State; Vice President of the United States

INTERESTING FACTS AND QUOTES

✦ His nickname of OK is a reference to his hometown Kinderhook; we have the saying "OK" as a result.

✦ He was the first president born an American citizen. All earlier presidents were born as British subjects.

✦ Hannah Van Buren was known for her concern for the poor. She died 18 years before her husband's election; he never remarried.

✦ The last sitting vice president to be elected to the presidency until George H. W. Bush in 1988.

✦ Opposed slavery and predicted it would end "amid convulsive" national consequences.

William Henry Harrison

9th President • March 4, 1841 - April 4, 1841

BIRTHDATE: February 9, 1773
BIRTHPLACE: Berkeley Plantation, Charles City County, Virginia
PHYSICAL DESCRIPTION: 5 ft. 8 in., slim
EDUCATION: Hampden-Sydney College; Philadelphia College of Physicians and Surgeons
RELIGION: Episcopalian
FIRST LADY: Anna Symmes Harrison
CHILDREN: Elizabeth, John Cleves, Lucy, William, John Scott, Benjamin, Mary, Carter, Anna, James
MILITARY SERVICE: Professional soldier
POLITICAL PARTY: Whig
VICE PRESIDENT: John Tyler
SALARY: $25,000/year
NICKNAME: Old Tippecanoe
DIED (IN OFFICE): April 4, 1841, in the White House
BURIED: Harrison tomb, North Bend, Ohio

ACCOMPLISHMENTS AND EVENTS

★ Only serving a month in office, he accomplished little as President. His previous distinguished public service and national hero status had led to his sweep of the electoral college in the election.

★ He saw his role as president to implement the will of the people.

★ He planned to end the spoils system as practiced by previous administrations.

★ BEFORE THE PRESIDENCY: Professional soldier; Secretary of the Northwest Territory; Northwest Territory Delegate to the U.S. House; Governor of Indiana Territory; Member, U.S. House of Representatives; Member, Ohio State Senate; Member, U.S. Senate; U.S. Minister to Columbia

INTERESTING FACTS AND QUOTES

✦ First president to die in office.

✦ He gave the longest inaugural address and served the shortest term.

✦ Grandfather of future president, Benjamin Harrison.

✦ Only occasion when both president and vice-president were born in the same county and served consecutive terms as president.

✦ Appointed Daniel Webster as his Secretary of State.

✦ **The oldest First Lady, Anna Harrison never came to the White House; her husband died before she could travel to Washington.**

"Those who are called upon to administer it [our democracy] must recognize as its leading principle the duty of shaping their measures so as to produce the greatest good for the greatest number."

23

Believed in making decisions based on principles and not on politics; at a party shortly before leaving office, he said: "They cannot say now that I am a president without a party."

John Tyler

10th President • April 6, 1841 - March 3, 1845

BIRTHDATE: March 29, 1790
BIRTHPLACE: Charles City County, Virginia
PHYSICAL DESCRIPTION: Just over 6 ft., thin
EDUCATION: College of William and Mary
RELIGION: Episcopalian
FIRST LADIES: Letitia Christian Tyler and Julia Gardiner Tyler
CHILDREN: Mary, Robert, John, Letitia, Elizabeth, Anne, Alice, Tazewell, David, John Alexander, Julia, Lachlan, Lyon, Robert Fitzgerald, Pearl
MILITARY SERVICE: Captain of the Charles City Rifles to defend Richmond during the War of 1812
POLITICAL PARTY: Democratic; Whig
VICE PRESIDENT: None
SALARY: $25,000/year
NICKNAME: His Accidency
DIED: January 18, 1862, in Richmond, Virginia
BURIED: Hollywood Cemetery, Richmond, Virginia

ACCOMPLISHMENTS AND EVENTS

★ Upon the death of President Harrison, Vice President John Tyler assumed the office of president, not of acting president, and in so doing clarified an ambiguity in the Constitution.

★ Nearly killed while inspecting the warship, USS Princeton; its main weapon, the world's largest naval gun, exploded, killing six men.

★ Preemption Act of 1841 - a bill recognizing squatters' rights to occupy public lands.

★ Signed the Webster-Ashburton Treaty which set the boundaries between the state of Maine and the Canadian province of New Brunswick.

★ He reorganized the U.S. Navy.

★ ADMITTED TO THE UNION: Florida

★ BEFORE THE PRESIDENCY: Lawyer; Member, Virginia House of Delegates; Member, U.S. House of Representatives; Governor of Virginia; Member, U.S. Senate

INTERESTING FACTS AND QUOTES

◆ As vice president for William Henry Harrison, this marked the only occasion when both president and vice president were born in the same county and served consecutive terms as president.

◆ He was born in 1790 and his grandson was alive in 2006.

◆ Letitia Tyler was the first president's wife to die in the White House.

◆ First president to marry while in office. Married Julia Gardiner who started the tradition of playing "Hail to the Chief" when the president attends state functions.

◆ Had 15 children (by two wives).

◆ After his presidency, he served in the Confederate government.

James Knox Polk

11th President • March 4, 1845 - March 3, 1849

BIRTHDATE: November 2, 1795
BIRTHPLACE: Mecklenberg County, North Carolina
PHYSICAL DESCRIPTION: 5 ft. 8 in., sturdily built
EDUCATION: University of North Carolina
RELIGION: Presbyterian and Methodist
FIRST LADY: Sarah Childress Polk
CHILDREN: None
MILITARY SERVICE: Commissioned as a captain of a militia cavalry regiment, later rising to colonel
POLITICAL PARTY: Democratic
VICE PRESIDENT: George M. Dallas
SALARY: $25,000/year
NICKNAME: Young Hickory
DIED: June 15, 1849, in Nashville, Tennessee
BURIED: State Capitol, Nashville, Tennessee

ACCOMPLISHMENTS AND EVENTS

★ Set the 49th parallel as the boundary between the United States and Canada.

★ Asked Congress for a declaration of war with Mexico. The U.S. won the war, fixing the border with Mexico at the Rio Grande; thus, the United States acquired more than 500,000 square miles in the Southwest, the largest land acquisition since the Louisiana Purchase.

★ Signed the Independent Treasury Act, requiring that all federal funds be deposited in treasuries that were not part of private banks.

★ Gold was discovered in California.

★ ADMITTED TO THE UNION: Texas, Iowa, Wisconsin

★ BEFORE THE PRESIDENCY: Lawyer; Member, Tennessee House of Representatives; Member, U.S. House of Representatives; Speaker of the House; Governor of Tennessee

INTERESTING FACTS AND QUOTES

✦ Had a gall bladder operation with no anesthesia at the age of 17.

✦ Married Sarah Childress after being encouraged in their romance by Andrew Jackson.

✦ Hosted the first Thanksgiving in the White House.

✦ A devout Presbyterian, Mrs. Polk banned dancing, card-playing, and alcoholic beverages from the White House.

✦ Authorized the Smithsonian Institution and established the Naval Academy.

✦ After his death, Mrs. Polk dressed in black everyday until her death 42 years later.

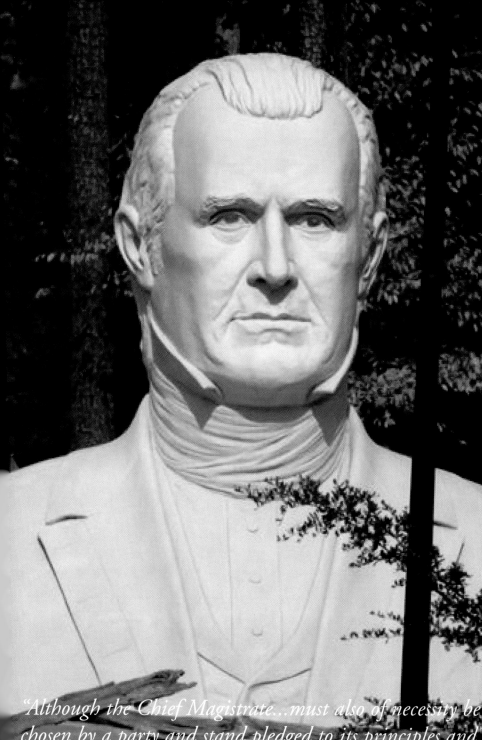

"Although the Chief Magistrate...must also of necessity be chosen by a party and stand pledged to its principles and measures, ... in his official action he should not be president of a party only, but of the whole people of the United States."

"*For more than half a century, during which kingdoms and empires have fallen, this Union has stood unshaken. The patriots who formed it have long descended into the grave; yet still it remains, the proudest monument to their memory...*"

Zachary Taylor

12th President • March 5, 1849 - July 9, 1850

BIRTHDATE: November 24, 1784
BIRTHPLACE: Montebello, Virginia
PHYSICAL DESCRIPTION: 5 ft. 8 in., 200 lbs.
EDUCATION: Slight formal education
RELIGION: Episcopalian
FIRST LADY: Margaret Smith Taylor
CHILDREN: Anne, Sarah, Octavia, Margaret, Mary, Richard
MILITARY SERVICE: Career military officer from 1808 to 1848
POLITICAL PARTY: Whig
VICE PRESIDENT: Millard Fillmore
SALARY: $25,000/year
NICKNAME: Old Rough and Ready
DIED (IN OFFICE): July 9, 1850, in the White House in Washington, D.C.
BURIED: Zachary Taylor National Cemetery, Louisville, Kentucky

ACCOMPLISHMENTS AND EVENTS

★ Known as the nation's most recognized Mexican War hero.

★ Signed the Clayton-Bulwer Treaty with England, providing that both countries would control any canal constructed across Central America, linking the Atlantic and Pacific Oceans.

★ Although a slaveholder himself, Taylor opposed the extension of slavery and was committed to the Union. He opposed the Compromise of 1850 because of its aspects favoring the South.

★ He vowed to stop states from secession, even if it meant war.

★ BEFORE THE PRESIDENCY: Distinguished military career in Louisiana; Commandant in Minnesota, Wisconsin, Arkansas, and the Mexican War

INTERESTING FACTS AND QUOTES

✦ A descendent of Williams Brewster, who arrived on the Mayflower; he was second cousin to James Madison and related to Robert E. Lee.

✦ Refusing to pay postage due, he did not accept the letter that contained his nomination to the Presidency by the Whig party.

✦ First president not previously elected to any other public office.

✦ In her 60s when her husband assumed office, Margaret Taylor was in ill health.

✦ Their second daughter was the first wife of Confederate President Jefferson Davis.

✦ Died unexpectedly in office; the second president to die in the White House.

Millard Fillmore

13th President • July 10, 1850 - March 4, 1853

BIRTHDATE: January 7, 1800
BIRTHPLACE: Locke Township (later Summerhill), New York
PHYSICAL DESCRIPTION: 5 ft. 9 in.
EDUCATION: Six months of grade school; studied law
RELIGION: Unitarian
FIRST LADY: Abigail Powers Fillmore
CHILDREN: Millard, Mary
MILITARY SERVICE: Organized a Buffalo military guard; held the rank of major
POLITICAL PARTY: Whig
VICE PRESIDENT: None
SALARY: $25,000/year
NICKNAME: Last of the Whigs
DIED: March 8, 1874, in Buffalo, New York
BURIED: Forest Lawn Cemetery, Buffalo, New York

ACCOMPLISHMENTS AND EVENTS

★ Signed Compromise of 1850, which was intended to prevent civil war. To placate the South, he enforced the Fugitive Slave Act, requiring the federal government to assist in returning fugitive slaves to their owners. Fillmore's action is credited with losing him the nomination for president in 1852.

★ Authorized Matthew J. Perry's trip to Japan; opened two Japanese ports to American trade.

★ ADMITTED TO THE UNION: California

★ BEFORE THE PRESIDENCY: Lawyer; Member, New York State Assembly; Member, U.S. House of Representatives; Comptroller of New York State; Vice President of the United States

INTERESTING FACTS AND QUOTES

✦ As vice president, he became president when Zachary Taylor unexpectedly died in office.

✦ He was an indentured servant to a cloth maker and finally bought his freedom for $30.00.

✦ An avid book lover, Abigail Fillmore established a library in the White House with Congressional funding; she also added a modern bathroom and an iron stove for cooking.

✦ As a state assemblyman, he fought unsuccessfully to abolish a New York law requiring witnesses in court to swear belief in God.

✦ Refused an honorary degree from Oxford University because he felt he had "neither literary nor scientific attainment."

"It is not strange to mistake change for progress."

"With the Union, my best and dearest earthly hopes are entwined."

Franklin Pierce

14th President • March 4, 1853 - March 3, 1857

BIRTHDATE: November 23, 1804
BIRTHPLACE: Hillsborough, New Hampshire
PHYSICAL DESCRIPTION: 5 ft. 10 in.
EDUCATION: Bowdoin College
RELIGION: Episcopalian
FIRST LADY: Jane Appleton Pierce, daughter of the President of Bowdoin College
CHILDREN: Franklin, Frank Robert, Benjamin
MILITARY SERVICE: Brigadier general; fought in the Mexican War
POLITICAL PARTY: Democratic
VICE PRESIDENT: William R. King
SALARY: $25,000/year
NICKNAME: Handsome Frank
DIED: October 8, 1869, in Concord, New Hampshire
BURIED: Old North Cemetery, Concord, New Hampshire

ACCOMPLISHMENTS AND EVENTS

★ Responsible for purchase of over 45,000 square miles of land from Mexico, now part of Arizona and New Mexico; this completed the modern outline of the 48 states.

★ Approved the Kansas-Nebraska Act, giving these territories the right to adopt slavery; led to the "Bleeding Kansas" conflict. Kansas became the site of bloody encounters including the infamous raid of John Brown.

★ Promoted idea of transcontinental railroad.

★ Appointed Jefferson Davis, future president of the Confederacy, to his cabinet as Secretary of War.

★ Signed Ostend Manifesto urging Spain to sell Cuba to the United States for $120 million.

★ BEFORE THE PRESIDENCY: Lawyer; Member, New Hampshire Legislature; Member, U.S. Senate; Member, U.S. House of Representatives

INTERESTING FACTS AND QUOTES

✦ Classmates in college included Nathaniel Hawthorne and Henry Wadsworth Longfellow.

✦ First president who opted to say "I solemnly affirm" in his inaugural oath instead of "I solemnly swear."

✦ Delivered entire 3,319 word inaugural address from memory without notes.

✦ Overcome with grief from seeing her son killed, Jane Pierce became known as "the shadow in the White House."

✦ Each of his children died before he became president.

✦ Appointed by Major General Winfield Scott to negotiate an armistice to end the Mexican War. Took part in the occupation of the Mexican capital in 1847.

James Buchanan

15th President • March 4, 1857 - March 3, 1861

BIRTHDATE: April 23, 1791
BIRTHPLACE: Cove Gap, Pennsylvania
PHYSICAL DESCRIPTION: A bit over 6 ft.
EDUCATION: Dickinson College
RELIGION: Presbyterian
FIRST LADIES: Never married; no children
MILITARY SERVICE: Served in the War of 1812
POLITICAL PARTY: Democratic
VICE PRESIDENT: John C. Breckinridge
SALARY: $25,000/year
NICKNAME: Old Buck
DIED: June 1, 1868, at his Wheatland estate in Lancaster, Pennsylvania
BURIED: Woodward Hill Cemetery, Lancaster, Pennsylvania

ACCOMPLISHMENTS AND EVENTS

★ The situation leading to Civil War intensified under his administration. The Dred
  Scott decision, holding that slaves and descendents were property and not citizens, was
  rendered by the U.S. Supreme Court; John Brown raided Harper's Ferry, Virginia, esca-
  lating fears of the South and abolitionist anger in the North.

★ Oversaw the economic depression that lasted until the Civil War.

★ Sent Army to Utah to put down a reported Mormon rebellion.

★ The Confederate States of America was formed under President Jefferson Davis (after
  Lincoln's election).

★ ADMITTED TO THE UNION: Minnesota, Oregon, Kansas

★ SECEDED FROM THE UNION: Alabama, Florida, Georgia, Louisiana, Mississippi,
  South Carolina, Texas

★ BEFORE THE PRESIDENCY: Lawyer; Member, Pennsylvania House of
  Representatives; Member, U.S. House of Representatives; U.S. Minister to Russia and to
  Great Britain; Member, U.S. Senate; Secretary of State

INTERESTING FACTS AND QUOTES

✦ Last president born in the eighteenth century and only president to have never married.

✦ At age 28, he was engaged to be married to Ann Coleman. She heard rumors that he
  was marrying her for her money and broke the engagement; she died soon thereafter. He
  wrote to her father asking to be a pallbearer at her funeral. The letter was returned
  unopened. He remained a bachelor for the next 50 years.

✦ Niece Harriet Lane, orphaned at age 11, was official hostess for her favorite uncle, the
  president.

✦ Purchased slaves in Washington, D.C. and freed them in Pennsylvania.

✦ "What is right and what is practicable are two different things."

He said to Abraham Lincoln, "My dear sir, if you are as happy in entering the White House as I shall feel on returning to Wheatland, you are a happy man indeed."

Abraham Lincoln

16th President • March 4, 1861 - April 15, 1865
Preserved the Union

BIRTHDATE: February 12, 1809
BIRTHPLACE: Hardin County (near Hodgenville), Kentucky
PHYSICAL DESCRIPTION: Our tallest president at 6 ft. 4 in., 180 lbs.
EDUCATION: Total schooling less than one year. Sought a better life through reading. Studied law and became a lawyer.
RELIGION: No formal affiliation
FIRST LADY: Mary Todd Lincoln
CHILDREN: Robert, Edward, William, Thomas (Tad)
MILITARY SERVICE: Enlisted in April 1832, elected captain of company of volunteers to fight in the Black Hawk War; reenlisted as a private in the mounted Independent Rangers. Reenlisted again in the Independent Spy Corps to track down Chief Black Hawk in the wilderness.

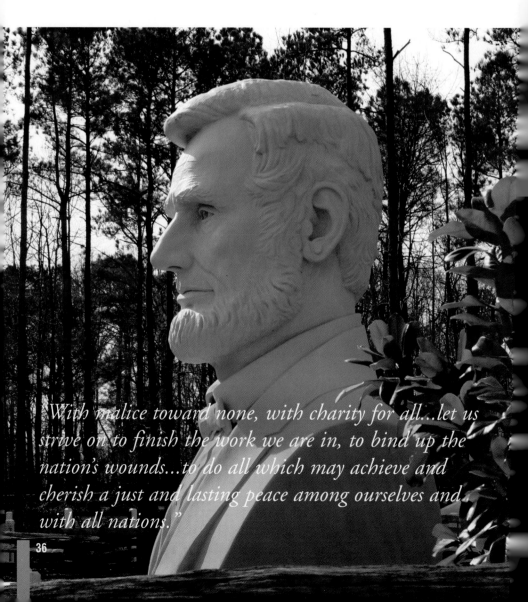

"With malice toward none, with charity for all...let us strive on to finish the work we are in, to bind up the nation's wounds...to do all which may achieve and cherish a just and lasting peace among ourselves and with all nations."

POLITICAL PARTY: Republican
BEFORE THE PRESIDENCY: Store clerk; Surveyor; Lawyer; Postmaster of New Salem, Illinois; Member, Illinois Legislature; Member, U.S. House of Representatives
VICE PRESIDENT: First term - Hannibal Hamlin
             Second term - Andrew Johnson
SALARY: $25,000/year
NICKNAME: Honest Abe, "Spotty" for criticizing government policy in the Mexican War
DIED (IN OFFICE): April 15, 1865, in Washington, D.C.
BURIED: Oak Ridge Cemetery, Springfield, Illinois

ACCOMPLISHMENTS AND EVENTS

★ Eleven states seceded from the Union in 1861 to form the Confederate States of America. As a result, Lincoln devoted his presidency to restoring the Union.

★ Issued the Emancipation Proclamation on January 1, 1863, declaring slavery unlawful in Confederate states still at war.

★ In 1862, signed the Homestead Act, granting160 acres of public land free to anybody willing to farm it for at least 5 years. Also signed the Morrill Act, granting to each state, proportionate to its representation in Congress, public lands, which were to be sold to finance agricultural and mechanical arts colleges.

★ He did not oppose the proposed Corwin Amendment to the Constitution, which would have prevented Congress from interfering with a state's "domestic institutions," including slavery. This amendment was never ratified.

★ On November 19, 1863, he delivered the Gettysburg Address.

★ ASSASSINATION: On April 14, 1865, while watching the performance of *Our American Cousin* at Ford's Theater in Washington, D.C., John Wilkes Booth shot President Lincoln in the back of the head with a .44 derringer. He was taken across the street to Peterson's Boarding House where he died.

★ ADMITTED TO THE UNION: West Virginia, Nevada

★ SECEDED FROM THE UNION: Virginia, Arkansas, North Carolina, Tennessee

INTERESTING FACTS AND QUOTES

✦ First president to be born outside the original thirteen colonies.

✦ First president to be photographed at his inauguration (1865). His assassin, John Wilkes Booth, can be seen in the picture, standing close to Lincoln.

✦ Mary Todd Lincoln, although an advocate of emancipation, suffered from persistent public attacks that she was disloyal to the Union and pro-Confederate, as were her Kentucky relatives. Her brother, half-brothers, and brothers-in-law fought in the Confederate army.

✦ Son William died in the White House at the age of 12. Mrs. Lincoln was devastated by the loss.

✦ "A house divided against itself cannot stand."

✦ "The monstrous injustice of slavery...deprives our republican example of its just influence in the world-enables the enemies of free institutions, with plausibility, to taunt us as hypocrites."

✦ When an opponent called him two-faced, he responded: "If I had two faces, do you think I would be wearing this one?"

✦ He was the first president to have a full beard.

✦ The night he was assassinated, his pocket contained a Confederate five-dollar bill.

Andrew Johnson

17th President • April 15, 1865 - March 3, 1869

BIRTHDATE: December 29, 1808
BIRTHPLACE: Raleigh, North Carolina
PHYSICAL DESCRIPTION: 5 ft. 10 in.
EDUCATION: Wife taught him to read and write
RELIGION: No formal affiliation
FIRST LADY: Eliza McCardle Johnson
CHILDREN: Martha, Charles, Mary, Robert, Andrew
MILITARY SERVICE: In 1862, President Lincoln appointed him military governor of Tennessee with the rank of brigadier general
POLITICAL PARTY: Democratic
VICE PRESIDENT: None
SALARY: $25,000/year
NICKNAME: Tennessee Tailor
DIED: July 31, 1875, in Carter County, Tennessee
BURIED: Andrew Johnson National Cemetery, Greeneville, Tennessee

ACCOMPLISHMENTS AND EVENTS

★ Established the U.S. Department of Agriculture, leading to the organization of the Grange.

★ Favored a rapid Reconstruction of the South that gave white southerners their full rights. Opposed equal voting rights for blacks.

★ Congress passed the Civil Rights Act of 1866 to protect Southern blacks, which was incorporated into the Fourteenth Amendment.

★ The United States purchased Alaska from Russia, a total of 586,412 square miles, for 7.2 million dollars.

★ During his administration, the transatlantic telegraph cable was completed.

★ CONSTITUTIONAL AMENDMENTS RATIFIED: The 13th Amendment, outlawing slavery and the 14th Amendment, extending citizenship to former slaves.

★ ADMITTED TO THE UNION: Nebraska

★ RE-ADMITTED: Tennessee, Arkansas, Florida, North Carolina, Louisiana, South Carolina, Alabama

★ BEFORE THE PRESIDENCY: Tailor, Mayor, Greeneville, Tennessee; Member, Tennessee House of Representatives; Member, Tennessee State Senate; Member, U.S. House of Representatives; Governor of Tennessee; Member, U.S. Senate; Military Governor of Tennessee; Vice President of the United States

INTERESTING FACTS AND QUOTES

✦ Born and raised in extreme poverty; an indentured servant, he ran away at the age of 15. A reward was offered for his return.

✦ The first president to be impeached, escaping removal from office by one vote.

✦ Eliza Johnson taught her husband writing and arithmetic when he was 17.

✦ He made his own clothes.

✦ His funeral instructions were that his body be draped in an American flag and a copy of the United States Constitution be placed under his head.

✦ Only president to be elected to the Senate after the presidency.

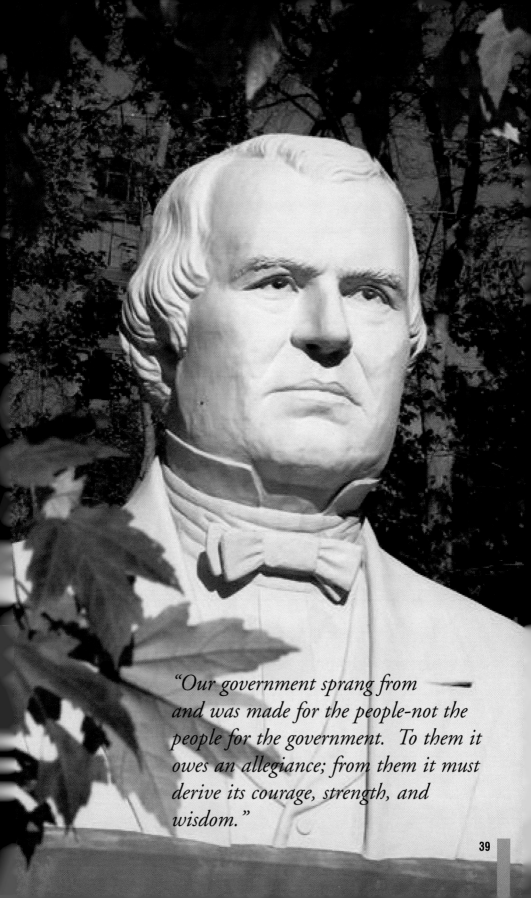

"Our government sprang from and was made for the people—not the people for the government. To them it owes an allegiance; from them it must derive its courage, strength, and wisdom."

39

"*The Southern Rebellion was largely the outgrowth of the Mexican War. Nations, like individuals, are punished for their transgressions. We got our punishment in the most sanguinary and expensive war of modern times.*"

Ulysses Simpson Grant

18th President • March 4, 1869 - March 3, 1877

BIRTHDATE: April 27, 1822
BIRTHPLACE: Point Pleasant, Ohio
PHYSICAL DESCRIPTION: 5 ft. 7 in., 150 lbs.
EDUCATION: U.S. Military Academy at West Point
RELIGION: Methodist
FIRST LADY: Julia Dent Grant
CHILDREN: Frederick, Ulysses, Ellen, Jesse
MILITARY SERVICE: Career military; commanded Union Armies during latter part of the Civil War
POLITICAL PARTY: Republican
VICE PRESIDENT: First term - Schuyler Colfax
                 Second term - Henry Wilson
SALARY: First term - $25,000/year
           Second term - $50,000/year
NICKNAME: Uncle Sam
DIED: July 23, 1885, in Mount McGregor, New York
BURIED: General Grant National Memorial, New York City

ACCOMPLISHMENTS AND EVENTS

★ After victories at Vicksburg and Lookout Mountain, he was made commander of all Union armies in March 1864. He received General Lee's formal surrender at Appomattox on April 9, 1865.

★ Threatened armed force against any state denying the right of blacks to vote and sent troops into the field to assist federal officials arresting members of organizations such as the Ku Klux Klan.

★ Panic of 1873 - A financial panic that led to a five year depression, resulted in three million people unemployed.

★ Established Yellowstone as the first national park.

★ CONSTITUTIONAL AMENDMENT RATIFIED: The 15th Amendment, granting the right to vote to men, without regards to color, race, or former slave status.

★ BEFORE THE PRESIDENCY: Service in the military

★ ADMITTED TO THE UNION: Colorado

★ RE-ADMITTED: Virginia, Mississippi, Texas, Georgia

INTERESTING FACTS AND QUOTES

✦ Volunteered to rejoin the army and fight for the Union when he was a clerk, age 39.

✦ He received a $20.00 ticket for speeding on his horse in Washington, D.C. Later the officer discovered that the speeder was the President of the United States.

✦ Julia Grant entertained lavishly in the White House; she was known as kindly and unassuming.

✦ First President to declare Christmas Day as a federal holiday.

✦ While Grant was suffering with throat cancer, Mark Twain helped him write his memoirs.

✦ Upon leaving the White House, apologized for errors of judgment, not for errors of intent.

Rutherford Birchard Hayes

19th President • March 4, 1877 - March 3, 1881

BIRTHDATE: October 4, 1822
BIRTHPLACE: Delaware, Ohio
PHYSICAL DESCRIPTION: 5 ft. 8 1/2 in., 170 lbs.
EDUCATION: Kenyon College; Harvard Law School
RELIGION: Presbyterian
FIRST LADY: Lucy Webb Hayes
CHILDREN: Birchard, Webb, Rutherford, Joseph, George, Fanny, Scott, Manning
MILITARY SERVICE: Major general in the Civil War
POLITICAL PARTY: Republican
VICE PRESIDENT: William A. Wheeler
SALARY: $50,000/year
NICKNAMES: His Fraudulency, Dark-Horse President
DIED: January 17, 1893, at Spiegel Grove in Fremont, Ohio
BURIED: Rutherford B. Hayes Presidential Center, Fremont, Ohio

ACCOMPLISHMENTS AND EVENTS

★ Ended Reconstruction by ordering federal troops to leave Statehouse grounds in Louisiana and South Carolina.

★ Issued executive order on civil service reform, barring federal employees from political activities; called for comprehensive civil service reform. Congress failed to act.

★ Authorized negotiation of the Treaty of 1880, restricting future Chinese immigration.

★ Set policy to have a canal through Central America under American control; this is the Panama Canal.

★ Signed legislation allowing women to practice law before the U.S. Supreme Court.

★ Restored respect for the presidency and aided the healing of the nation's wounds from the Civil War.

★ BEFORE THE PRESIDENCY: Lawyer; Member, U.S. House of Representatives; Governor of Ohio.

INTERESTING FACTS AND QUOTES

✦ As a child, won spelling contests in school.

✦ During Civil War, served with the 23rd Ohio Infantry. Wounded five times, once seriously; horse shot from under him four times.

✦ Won presidency by one electoral vote even though he lost the popular vote by approximately 250,000 votes.

✦ Banned use of alcohol in the White House in order to bring members of the Prohibition Party back into the Republican fold.

✦ Lucy Hayes was first First Lady with college degree. She was well-liked, intelligent, warm, and gracious.

✦ Telephone and typewriter were first used in the White House during Hayes' presidency; telephone was installed by Alexander Graham Bell.

✦ First president to visit the West Coast while in office.

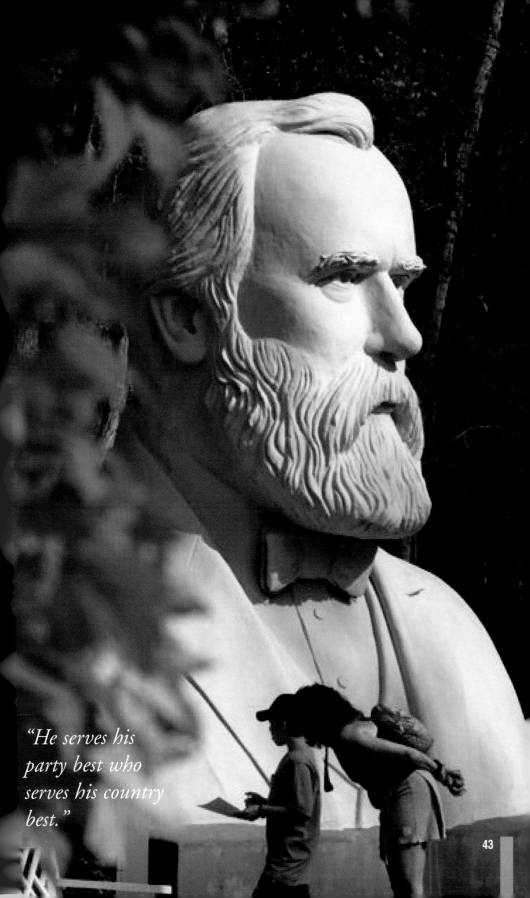

"He serves his party best who serves his country best."

"*A brave man is a man who dares to look the Devil in the face and tell him he is a Devil.*"

44

James Abram Garfield

20th President • March 4, 1881 - September 19, 1881

BIRTHDATE: November 19, 1831
BIRTHPLACE: Cuyahoga County, Ohio
PHYSICAL DESCRIPTION: 6 ft., 185 lbs.
EDUCATION: Eclectic Institute (now Hiram College); Williams College
RELIGION: Disciples of Christ
FIRST LADY: Lucretia Rudolph Garfield
CHILDREN: Eliza, Harry, James, Mollie, Irvin, Abram, Edward
MILITARY SERVICE: Youngest brigadier general in the Union Army during the Civil War
POLITICAL PARTY: Republican
VICE PRESIDENT: Chester A. Arthur
SALARY: $50,000/year
NICKNAME: Preacher President
DIED (IN OFFICE): September 19, 1881, Elberon, New Jersey
BURIED: Lake View Cemetery, Cleveland, Ohio

ACCOMPLISHMENTS AND EVENTS

★ Star Route Scandal: Ordered investigation of charges that mail route contracts were being fraudulently awarded. Inquiry indicated bribery involving members of his own party. Several were implicated but no one was convicted. Scandal led eventually to civil service reform.

★ American Red Cross organized under the leadership of Clara Barton.

★ In spite of short presidency, he had a long and distinguished career of public service, serving 17 years in the U.S. House before election as Senator from Ohio. He was elected president before he could take his Senate seat. He is remembered for moving the nation toward the elimination of political patronage.

★ BEFORE THE PRESIDENCY: Teacher; College president; Lawyer; Member, Ohio State Senate; Member, U.S. House of Representatives

INTERESTING FACTS AND QUOTES

✦ Wrote Latin with one hand and Greek with the other, both at the same time.
✦ Last president born in a log cabin.
✦ His mother was the first mother of a president to witness the inauguration.
✦ Active lay minister in his church and known as the only preacher to become president.
✦ ASSASSINATION: Shot July 2, 1881, four months after taking office, by a deranged lawyer who wanted to be named Ambassador to France; Garfield died ten weeks later.
✦ First Lady Lucretia Garfield fell gravely ill from malaria and was recovering in New Jersey when her husband was shot.

Chester Alan Arthur

21st President • September 20, 1881 - March 3, 1885

BIRTHDATE: October 5, 1830
BIRTHPLACE: North Fairfield, Vermont
PHYSICAL DESCRIPTION: 6 ft. 2 in., 225 lbs.
EDUCATION: Union College
RELIGION: Episcopalian
FIRST LADY: Ellen Herndon Arthur
CHILDREN: William, Chester, Jr., Ellen
MILITARY SERVICE: Quartermaster General in New York State militia during the Civil War
POLITICAL PARTY: Republican
VICE PRESIDENT: None
SALARY: $50,000/year
NICKNAME: Elegant Arthur, The Gentleman Boss, Dude President
DIED: November 18, 1886, at his home in New York City
BURIED: Albany Rural Cemetery, Albany, New York

ACCOMPLISHMENTS AND EVENTS

★ Signed Chinese Exclusion Act, suspended Chinese immigration, and forbade granting of citizenship to Chinese immigrants already in the United States. Although renewed in 1892 and 1902, this law was repealed in 1943.

★ Signed Pendleton Act, creating the modern civil service system, including a Civil Service Commission; featured open, competitive exams and banned the practice of exacting political contributions from civil servants.

★ Credited with eliminating the corruption of patronage from the Republican Party.

★ Enacted first federal immigration law to keep criminals and insane people from coming into the United States from other countries.

★ BEFORE THE PRESIDENCY: Teacher; Lawyer; Collector of Port of New York; Vice President of the United States.

INTERESTING FACTS AND QUOTES

✦ Son of a fervent abolitionist Baptist minister.

✦ Became president upon the death of President Garfield.

✦ Ellen Lewis Herndon Arthur, at the age of 42, died of pneumonia ten months before her husband was elected vice president.

✦ As president, attended St. John's Episcopal Church in Washington, to which he donated a stained-glass window in memory of his late wife. It was placed so that he could see it from the White House.

✦ Dedicated the Washington Monument on February 21, 1885.

"Since I came here I have learned that Chester A. Arthur is one man and the President of the United States is another."

47

"Officeholders are the agents of the people, not their masters."

Steven Grover Cleveland

22nd President • 24th President
March 4, 1885 - March 3, 1889   March 4, 1893 - March 3, 1897

BIRTHDATE: March 18, 1837
BIRTHPLACE: Caldwell, New Jersey
PHYSICAL DESCRIPTION: 5 ft. 11 in., 250 lbs.
EDUCATION: Some school; studied law
RELIGION: Presbyterian
FIRST LADY: Frances Folsom Cleveland
CHILDREN: Ruth, Esther, Marion, Richard, Francis
MILITARY SERVICE: None
POLITICAL PARTY: Democratic
VICE PRESIDENT: First Term -Thomas A. Hendricks
             Second Term - Adlai E. Stevenson
SALARY: $50,000/year
NICKNAME: Uncle Jumbo
DIED: June 24, 1908, at his home Westland in Princeton, New Jersey
BURIED: Princeton Cemetery, Princeton, New Jersey

ACCOMPLISHMENTS AND EVENTS

FIRST TERM
★ Signed Interstate Commerce Act, creating the Interstate Commerce Commission, the first federal regulatory agency.
★ Signed Dawes Severalty Act, granting citizenship and full title of reservation land to Indians willing to renounce tribal allegiance.
★ Signed Hatch Act, providing federal funds to establish experiment stations under the direction of agricultural colleges in various states.

SECOND TERM
★ Four-year depression beginning with the Panic of 1893.
★ Sent federal troops to end the Pullman Strike of 1894, which had crippled rail traffic between Chicago and the West Coast.
★ ADMITTED TO THE UNION: Utah
★ BEFORE THE PRESIDENCY: Lawyer; Sheriff of Erie County, New York; Mayor of Buffalo, New York; Governor of New York

INTERESTING FACTS AND QUOTES

✦ Worked as a clerk in a store for $50.00 a year plus room and board.
✦ Only president to be married in the White House. She was 21 and he was 49. When asked why he did not marry her sooner, he replied that he had to wait for her to grow up.
✦ He was drafted during the Civil War but chose to purchase a substitute, a legal option.
✦ Only president to serve two non-consecutive terms.
✦ The Baby Ruth candy bar is named after his daughter, Ruth.
✦ "He mocks the people who proposes that the government shall protect the rich and that they, in turn, will care for the laboring poor."

Benjamin Harrison

23rd President • March 4, 1889 - March 3, 1893

BIRTHDATE: August 20, 1833
BIRTHPLACE: North Bend, Ohio
PHYSICAL DESCRIPTION: 5 ft. 6 in.
EDUCATION: Miami University, Oxford, Ohio
RELIGION: Presbyterian
FIRST LADY: Caroline Scott Harrison
CHILDREN: Russell, Mary, Elizabeth
MILITARY SERVICE: Organized 70th Regiment of Volunteers of Indiana during the Civil War
POLITICAL PARTY: Republican
VICE PRESIDENT: Levi P. Morton
SALARY: $50,000/year
NICKNAME: Little Ben, The Human Iceberg
DIED: March 13, 1901, in Indianapolis, Indiana
BURIED: Crown Hill Cemetery, Indianapolis, Indiana

ACCOMPLISHMENTS AND EVENTS

★ Signed bills that set aside the first urban park-Rock Creek Park in Washington, D.C.— and the first prehistoric Indian ruins to come under federal protection.

★ Approved legislation that set aside more than 13 million acres of land for national forest reserves.

★ Established practice of daily display of the American flag over public buildings and schools.

★ Tried to get a law passed to stop the frequent lynching of blacks.

★ Signed the Dependent and Disability Pensions Act, extending compensation to veterans disabled from nonmilitary causes and to dependents. Also signed the Sherman Anti-Trust Act.

★ Hired the first woman to work in the White House in a position other than domestic service; appointed black postmasters in large southern cities.

★ ADMITTED TO THE UNION: North Dakota, South Dakota, Montana, Washington, Idaho, Wyoming

★ BEFORE THE PRESIDENCY: Lawyer; Supreme Court Reporter; Member, U.S. Senate

INTERESTING FACTS AND QUOTES

✦ The family's history of public service is one of the most impressive in U.S. history. His great-grandfather signed the Declaration of Independence and his grandfather was ninth president of the U.S.

✦ He had eleven family members living in the White House with only one bathroom.

✦ Spent so many evenings courting his wife that he was nicknamed "the moonlight dude."

✦ Only president to be preceded and succeeded by the same president.

✦ Caroline Harrison, first President General of the DAR, raised funds for the Johns Hopkins University Medical School on the condition that women be admitted. She was one of five First Ladies to die in the White House.

"Great lives do not go out, they go on."

51

"That's all a man can hope for during his lifetime-to set an example-and when he is dead, to be an inspiration for history."

52

William McKinley

25th President • March 4, 1897 - September 14, 1901

BIRTHDATE: January 29, 1843
BIRTHPLACE: Niles, Ohio
PHYSICAL DESCRIPTION: 5 ft. 7 in., nearly 200 lbs.
EDUCATION: Allegheny College; Albany Law School
RELIGION: Methodist
FIRST LADY: Ida Saxton McKinley
CHILDREN: Katherine, Ida
MILITARY SERVICE: Served with 23rd Ohio Volunteer Infantry in the Civil War
POLITICAL PARTY: Republican
VICE PRESIDENT: First term - Garret A. Hobart
　　　　　　　　Second term - Theodore Roosevelt
SALARY: $50,000/year
NICKNAME: Wobbly Willie, Front Porch Campaigner
DIED (IN OFFICE): September 14, 1901, in Buffalo, New York
BURIED: McKinley National Memorial and Museum, Canton, Ohio

ACCOMPLISHMENTS AND EVENTS

★ Joint congressional resolution annexed the Hawaiian Islands and Samoa.

★ Spanish-American War was declared after an explosion destroyed the U.S. Battleship *Maine*, which sank in Havana harbor, killing 266 of the crew.

★ The war lasted two years; under the terms of the peace, Spain relinquished its claim to Cuba and ceded Puerto Rico, Guam, and the Philippine Islands to the United States.

★ Sent American troops to China to suppress the Boxer Rebellion.

★ Signed Gold Standard Act, providing that the nation formally place money on the gold standard.

★ BEFORE THE PRESIDENCY: Lawyer; County prosecutor; Member, U.S. House of Representatives; Governor of Ohio

INTERESTING FACTS AND QUOTES

✦ Wore a scarlet carnation in his lapel as a good luck charm.

✦ Last president to have served in the Civil War.

✦ ASSASSINATION: On September 6, 1901, McKinley was shot while shaking hands at a public event; the assassin was an unemployed mill worker who viewed politicians as enemies of the working class.

✦ On being shot, he cried out to his guards, "Don't let them hurt him (the assassin)."

✦ Ida McKinley had become paralyzed and suffered from seizures.

✦ "Our differences are politics. Our agreements are principles."

Theodore Roosevelt

26th President • September 14, 1901 - March 3, 1909
"Speak softly and carry a big stick."

BIRTHDATE: October 27, 1858
BIRTHPLACE: New York City, New York
PHYSICAL DESCRIPTION: 5 ft. 8 in., 200 lbs.
EDUCATION: Harvard College
RELIGION: Dutch Reformed
FIRST LADY: Alice Hathaway Lee Roosevelt
               Edith Kermit Carow Roosevelt
CHILDREN: Alice, Theodore, Jr., Kermit, Ethel, Archibald, Quentin
MILITARY SERVICE: Member of New York National Guard; during the Spanish-American War, served as commander of the First U.S. Volunteer Cavalry Regiment, known as the Rough Riders. He became famous for his charge on San Juan Hill.
POLITICAL PARTY: Republican
BEFORE THE PRESIDENCY: Member, New York State Assembly; Member of U.S. Civil Service Commission; President of New York City Police Board; Assistant Secretary of the Navy; Governor of New York; Vice President of the United States
VICE PRESIDENT: Charles W. Fairbanks
SALARY: $50,000/year
NICKNAME: TR, Trust-Buster, Teddy
DIED: January 6, 1919, at his home, Sagamore Hill, in Oyster Bay, Long Island, New York
BURIED: Young's Memorial Cemetery, Oyster Bay, New York

ACCOMPLISHMENTS AND EVENTS

★ First controversial presidential act was inviting Booker T. Washington to dinner at the White House; set off white riots in the South that killed blacks.

★ Enforced anti-trust legislation, limiting the power of monopoly businesses and opposing child labor.

★ Responsible for the construction of the Panama Canal.

★ Stated the obligation of the United States to enforce the Monroe Doctrine. His insistence on U.S. supremacy in the western hemisphere was part of the Big Stick Diplomacy.

★ The antitrust policy and advocacy of labor and consumer rights constituted the Square Deal.

★ Signed the Meat Inspection Act and the Pure Food and Drug Act, providing for government inspection of meat and barring certain foods, drugs, medicines, and liquors from interstate commerce.

★ The Great Conservationist: reserved 125 million acres in national forests, 68 million acres of coal land and 2,500 water-power sites. Doubled the number of national parks and created 16 national monuments. Established 51 wildlife refuges and Devils Tower in Wyoming as the first national monument.

★ Favored expanded federal role in regulatory and welfare programs; supported U.S. entrance into World War I, but opposed concept of the League of Nations.

★ Reached gentleman's agreement with Japan that they would curb emigration of laborers and the United States would not enact an exclusion law.

★ Mediator in Russo-Japanese War; accepted Japanese control of Korea.

★ ADMITTED TO THE UNION: Oklahoma

INTERESTING FACTS AND QUOTES

✦ Assumed office upon the assassination of McKinley.

✦ Third vice president in less than four decades to become president because the chief executive had been assassinated.

✦ Only president to receive the Congressional Medal of Honor.

✦ His wife, Alice, died following the birth of their daughter; his mother died of typhoid fever the same day, February 14, 1884.

✦ He married his childhood sweetheart, Edith, two years later.

✦ ASSASSINATION ATTEMPT: On his way to give a speech, he was shot. The bullet penetrated copies of his speech and his eyeglass case and fractured his 4th rib. With blood running down his shirt, he delivered the hour-long speech before going to the hospital.

✦ One of three presidents who won the Nobel Peace Prize.

✦ A member of the Dutch Reformed Church, he attended Episcopal services with his wife. He taught Sunday school there until the rector found out he was not Episcopalian and dismissed him.

✦ A firm believer in separation of church and state, he considered it unconstitutional and sacrilegious to stamp In God We Trust on U.S. coins; tried unsuccessfully to have it removed.

✦ Wrote thirty-five books, including the highly-acclaimed *The Winning of the West*.

✦ "It is hard to fail, but it is far worse never to have tried to succeed."

"Order without liberty and liberty without order are equally destructive."

"Next to the right of liberty, the right of property is the most important right guaranteed by the Constitution and the one which, united with that of personal liberty, has contributed more to the growth of civilization than any other institution established by the human race."

William Howard Taft

27th President • March 4, 1909 - March 3, 1913

BIRTHDATE: September 15, 1857
BIRTHPLACE: Cincinnati, Ohio
PHYSICAL DESCRIPTION: 6 ft. 2 in., 332 lbs.
EDUCATION: Yale College; Cincinnati Law School
RELIGION: Unitarian
FIRST LADY: Helen Herron Taft
CHILDREN: Robert, Helen, Charles
MILITARY SERVICE: None
POLITICAL PARTY: Republican
VICE PRESIDENT: James S. Sherman
SALARY: $75,000/year
NICKNAME: Big Bill
DIED: March 8, 1930, at his home in Washington, D.C.
BURIED: Arlington National Cemetery, Arlington, Virginia

ACCOMPLISHMENTS AND EVENTS

★ Signed the Mann-Elkins Act, extending the authority of the Interstate Commerce Commission to fix minimum rates charged by railroads.

★ Enforced the dismantling of the American Tobacco Company and the Standard Oil Company.

★ Signed act barring the interstate transportation of liquor into states where liquor is banned.

★ CONSTITUTIONAL AMENDMENT RATIFIED: The 16th Amendment, establishing the power of the federal government to tax income.

★ ADMITTED TO THE UNION: New Mexico and Arizona. Taft was the first president of the 48 contiguous states.

★ BEFORE THE PRESIDENCY: Lawyer; Tax collector; Judge, Cincinnati Superior Court; U.S. Solicitor General; Judge, Sixth U.S. Circuit Court; Dean, University of Cincinnati Law School; Commissioner and Governor-General of the Philippines; Secretary of War

INTERESTING FACTS AND QUOTES

✦ Having once been stuck in a normal size bathtub, he had an oversized bathtub installed in the White House. He weighed approximately 332 lbs.

✦ Started the tradition of throwing out the first baseball at the start of the season.

✦ Helen Taft helped establish the Cincinnati Symphony Orchestra; as First Lady, she requested that Japanese cherry trees be planted around the Tidal Basin.

✦ First president to serve as Chief Justice of the U.S. Supreme Court.

✦ First presidential funeral to be broadcast to the nation via radio.

Woodrow Wilson

28th President • March 4, 1913 - March 3, 1921
Presided over the Nation during World War I

BIRTHDATE: December 28, 1856
BIRTHPLACE: Staunton, Virginia; his father was a Presbyterian minister who served as a Chaplain in the Confederate army.
PHYSICAL DESCRIPTION: 5 ft. 11 in., 180 lbs.
EDUCATION: College of New Jersey (now Princeton University); University of Virginia Law School; Johns Hopkins University, Ph.D.
RELIGION: Presbyterian
FIRST LADIES: Ellen Louise Axson Wilson
                       Edith Bolling Galt Wilson
CHILDREN: Margaret, Jessie, Eleanor
MILITARY SERVICE: None
BEFORE THE PRESIDENCY: College Professor; President of Princeton University; Governor of New Jersey
POLITICAL PARTY: Democratic
VICE PRESIDENT: Thomas R. Marshall
SALARY: $75,000/year
NICKNAME: Professor
DIED: February 3, 1924, at his home in Washington, D.C.
BURIED: National Cathedral, Washington, D.C.

ACCOMPLISHMENTS AND EVENTS

★ Signed into law the Federal Reserve Act, creating the Federal Reserve System; created the Federal Trade Commission to investigate business practices of interstate corporations.

★ Signed the Clayton Anti-Trust Act, exempting labor and agricultural associations from antitrust laws.

★ Set the stage for the eight-hour work day by signing the Adamson Act.

★ Worked for laws to stop child labor and allowing workers to strike.

★ Maintained neutrality in early days of World War I, insisting on America's right as a neutral nation to trade with both sides, Great Britain and Germany. Ultimately this failed and the U.S. entered the war on the side of the British in order to shape the postwar world through the League of Nations that would promote representative governments.

★ Effective in negotiating the Treaty of Versailles, ending the War and establishing the League of Nations. Senate blocked U.S. ratification of the treaty and membership in the League.

★ His Fourteen Points for a lasting peace provided the foundation of the peace treaty and the League of Nations.

★ Established the National Park Service.

★ CONSTITUTIONAL AMENDMENTS RATIFIED: 17th Amendment, providing for the election of U.S. senators directly by the people; the 18th Amendment, prohibiting alcoholic beverages; and the 19th Amendment, extending to women the right to vote.

INTERESTING FACTS AND QUOTES

✦ Had some difficulty learning to read; persisted and became a clear, forceful writer.

✦ The only president to earn a Ph.D., his dissertation was the first of a series of brilliant writings on government.

✦ One of three presidents who won the Nobel Peace Prize.

- First president to speak to the nation by means of radio.
- Believed the number "13" was his lucky number. Dropped first name "Thomas" so that Woodrow and Wilson would equal 13 letters.
- **His first wife, Ellen, petitioned Congress on behalf of the poor; she died in the White House. His second wife, Edith, managed the affairs of state after he had a massive stroke.**
- "My earliest recollection is of standing in my father's gateway in Augusta, Georgia, when I was four years old, and hearing someone pass by and say that Mr. Lincoln was elected and there was to be war."
- "The Americans who went to Europe to die are a unique breed. Never before have men crossed the seas to a foreign land to fight for a cause which they did not pretend was peculiarly their own, which they knew was the cause of humanity and mankind. These Americans gave the greatest of all gifts, the gift of life and the gift of spirit."
- "Sometimes people call me an idealist. Well, that is the way I know I am an American."

"The business of government is justice."

"*We want the cradle of American childhood rocked under conditions so wholesome and so hopeful that no blight may touch it in its development, and we want to provide that no selfish interest, no material necessity, no lack of opportunity shall prevent the gaining of that education so essential to best citizenship.*"

Warren Gamaliel Harding

29th President • March 4, 1921 - August 2, 1923

BIRTHDATE: November 2, 1865
BIRTHPLACE: Corsica, Ohio
PHYSICAL DESCRIPTION: 6 ft.; he wore a size 14 shoe.
EDUCATION: Ohio Central College
RELIGION: Baptist
FIRST LADY: Florence DeWolfe Harding
CHILDREN: None
MILITARY SERVICE: None
POLITICAL PARTY: Republican
VICE PRESIDENT: Calvin Coolidge
SALARY: $75,000/year
NICKNAME: Wobbly Warren
DIED (IN OFFICE): August 2, 1923, in San Francisco, California
BURIED: Harding Tomb, Marion, Ohio

ACCOMPLISHMENTS AND EVENTS

★ Teapot Dome and other scandals characterized his administration.

★ Members of his administration were charged with accepting bribes, skimming proceeds from the sale of war surplus goods, kickbacks, and selling alcohol and drugs from veterans' hospitals. Several committed suicide.

★ Signed the treaty that formally ended World War I.

★ Refused U.S. entrance into the League of Nations.

★ Established the Bureau of the Budget, placing formal budgetary restraints on federal expenditures.

★ Pardoned Eugene V. Debs, leader of the Socialist party.

★ First president since the Civil War to speak out on southern soil for the rights of blacks.

★ BEFORE THE PRESIDENCY: Insurance salesman; Reporter; Newspaper publisher; Member, Ohio State Senate; Lieutenant Governor of Ohio; Member, U.S. Senate

INTERESTING FACTS AND QUOTES

✦ Florence Harding had a child by a previous marriage; the First Lady's father opposed the marriage to Harding, considering him inferior socially.

✦ First president to win an election in which American women could vote.

✦ First president to ride in a car to his inauguration.

✦ First president to visit Alaska.

Calvin Coolidge

30th President • August 3, 1923 - March 3, 1929

BIRTHDATE: July 4, 1872
BIRTHPLACE: Plymouth Notch, Vermont
PHYSICAL DESCRIPTION: 5 ft. 9 in.
EDUCATION: Amherst College
RELIGION: **Congregationalist**
FIRST LADY: **Grace Goodhue Coolidge**
CHILDREN: John, Calvin
MILITARY SERVICE: None
POLITICAL PARTY: Republican
VICE PRESIDENT: Charles G. Dawes
SALARY: $75,000/year
NICKNAME: Silent Cal
DIED: January 5, 1933, at his home, The Beeches, in Northampton, Massachusetts
BURIED: Plymouth Cemetery, Plymouth, Vermont

ACCOMPLISHMENTS AND EVENTS

★ Cleaned house of those implicated in Teapot Dome scandals; restored confidence in the executive branch of government.

★ Signed Immigration Act of 1924, excluding the Japanese from immigration to the U.S. and favoring immigration of northern Europeans.

★ Signed Tax Reduction - Revenue Acts, reducing taxes imposed during World War I.

★ Charles Lindbergh made his famous flight.

★ The first two commercial airline routes were approved.

★ Supported Kellogg-Briand Pact outlawing war, signed by sixty-three countries.

★ Babe Ruth hit 60 home runs.

★ BEFORE THE PRESIDENCY: Lawyer; Mayor of Northampton, Massachusetts; Member, Massachusetts State Senate and Senate President; Lieutenant Governor and Governor of Massachusetts; Vice President of the United States

INTERESTING FACTS AND QUOTES

✦ As vice president, he became president upon the death of President Harding. He was administered the oath of office by his father, a justice of the peace and notary public.

✦ First president to broadcast on radio from the White House.

✦ He was very quiet and shy. When a lady at a dinner party informed him that she had a wager that she could make him say more than two words, he replied, "You lose."

✦ **Grace Coolidge received an honorary Doctor of Laws degree from Boston University.**

✦ "If you don't say anything, you won't be called on to repeat it."

✦ "We cannot do everything at once, but we can do something at once."

"I have noticed that nothing I never said ever did me any harm."

"The worst evil of disregard for some law is that it destroys respect for all law."

Herbert Clark Hoover

31st President • March 4, 1929 - March 3, 1933

BIRTHDATE: August 10, 1874
BIRTHPLACE: West Branch, Iowa
EDUCATION: Stanford University
RELIGION: Society of Friends (Quaker)
FIRST LADY: Lou Henry Hoover
CHILDREN: Herbert, Jr., Allan
MILITARY SERVICE: None
POLITICAL PARTY: Republican
VICE PRESIDENT: Charles Curtis
SALARY: $75,000/year - refused by Hoover
NICKNAME: Chief
DIED: October 20, 1964 in New York, New York
BURIED: Herbert Hoover Library and Birthplace, West Branch, Iowa

ACCOMPLISHMENTS AND EVENTS

★ Signed Agricultural Marketing Act creating the Federal Farm Board to provide relief to farmers.

★ Stock market crashed and the Great Depression followed. By the spring of 1930, four million were unemployed; this number tripled by 1933. Hoover failed to grasp the enormity of the Depression.

★ In 1930, signed into law the Cramton Bill which created the Colonial National Monument, which became the Colonial Parkway joining Jamestown, Williamsburg, and Yorktown.

★ CONSTITUTIONAL AMENDMENT RATIFIED: 20th Amendment, reducing the time when non-elected public officials would be making laws, moving up presidential inauguration and authorized each new Congress to convene on January 3.

★ BEFORE THE PRESIDENCY: Led relief efforts during World War I; Secretary of Commerce

INTERESTING FACTS AND QUOTES

✦ First president born west of the Mississippi.

✦ Orphaned as a child, he was a self-made millionaire who refused a salary as president.

✦ **Both he and his wife were engineers and spoke fluent Chinese; she was the first woman to receive a degree in geology from Stanford and among the first in the U.S.**

✦ Raised a billion dollars for food and medicine during World War I. Fed millions of people in Europe; classified by the Germans as a man who would not be detained for any reason.

✦ Served in the government for 42 years and accepted no salary.

✦ **First Quaker president.**

✦ Second president who chose to "affirm" rather than to "swear" his inaugural oath.

✦ After his presidency, he headed the Famine Emergency Commission which ensured that food arrived to feed millions in countries nearly destroyed by war.

Franklin Delano Roosevelt

32nd President • March 4, 1933 - April 12, 1945
"The only thing we have to fear is fear itself."

BIRTHDATE: January 30, 1882

BIRTHPLACE: Hyde Park, New York. (Fifth cousin of President Theodore Roosevelt, whom he greatly admired although they were of different political parties.)

PHYSICAL DESCRIPTION: 6 ft. 1 in., 180 lbs.

EDUCATION: Harvard College

RELIGION: Episcopalian

FIRST LADY: Anna Eleanor Roosevelt

CHILDREN: Anna, James, Franklin, Elliot, Franklin Delano, Jr., John

MILITARY SERVICE: None. During World War I, he requested active duty, but President Wilson insisted he remain at his post as Assistant Secretary of the Navy.

POLITICAL PARTY: Democratic

BEFORE THE PRESIDENCY: Member New York State Senate; Assistant Secretary of the Navy; Governor of New York

VICE PRESIDENT: First and second terms - John N. Garner
Third term - Henry A. Wallace
Fourth term - Harry S Truman

SALARY: $75,000/year

NICKNAME: FDR

DIED (IN OFFICE): April 12, 1945, in Warm Springs, Georgia

BURIED: Franklin Roosevelt Library and Museum, Hyde Park, New York

ACCOMPLISHMENTS AND EVENTS

★ New Deal: Developed programs to bring the nation out of the Great Depression. Hired three million young men from poor families to do conservation work, established the Tennessee Valley Authority, the Public Works Administration, the National Recovery Administration, the Securities and Exchange Commission, the National Housing Act, the Social Security Act, and championed other social net legislation for families and children.

★ Signed the Hatch Act of 1939 prohibiting federal employees from engaging in partisan political activity.

★ Hoped to expand American trade with Russia and other nations in an effort to end the Great Depression.

★ Established formal diplomatic relations with the Soviet Union. The Soviets agreed to cease propaganda and subversive activities in the United States and to guarantee religious freedom and the right to fair trials to all Americans residing there.

★ The day after the attack on Pearl Harbor, Roosevelt asked Congress for a declaration of war.

★ Forcibly interned Japanese American citizens during World War II.

★ On June 6, 1944, General Eisenhower landed at Normandy enabling the liberation of Paris and leading to the end of the war.

★ Sought military bases in strategic areas of the world in order to have an offensive military capability that would quickly squash aggressors.

★ ASSASSINATION ATTEMPT: While president-elect, an assassination attempt in Miami was foiled; assassin was executed.

★ CONSTITUTIONAL AMENDMENT RATIFIED: 21st Amendment, providing for the repeal of Prohibition.

INTERESTING FACTS AND QUOTES

✦ Stricken with polio at the age of 39.

✦ **First Lady Eleanor Roosevelt, niece of President Theodore Roosevelt who gave her away in marriage, was an acclaimed social activist and advocate for those less fortunate. She sought equal pay for women.**

✦ First president to be elected to four terms.

✦ First president to appoint a female cabinet member; Frances Perkins served as Secretary of Labor.

✦ "Fireside Chats" on the radio were so popular that at times eighty percent of American households were listening.

✦ Declared December 7, 1941, the date of the Japanese attack on Pearl Harbor, as a day which "will live in infamy."

✦ "Let us never forget that government is ourselves and not an alien power over us. The ultimate rulers of our democracy are not a president or senators or congressmen and government officials, but the voters of this country."

✦ "The test of our progress is not whether we add abundance to those who have much, but whether we provide enough for those who have little."

✦ "We have always known that heedless self-interest was bad morals; we now know it is bad economics."

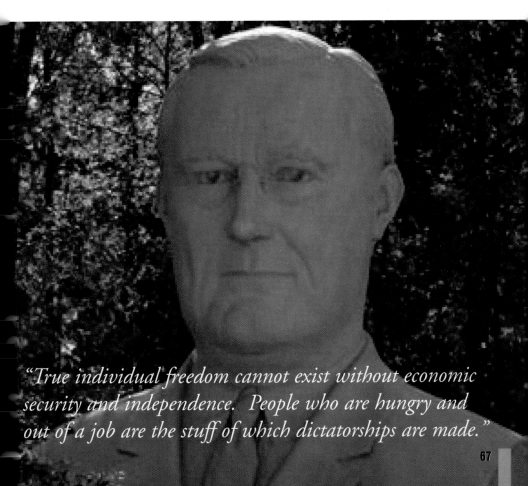

"True individual freedom cannot exist without economic security and independence. People who are hungry and out of a job are the stuff of which dictatorships are made."

"*Being a president is like riding a tiger. A man has to keep riding or be swallowed.*"

Harry S Truman

33rd President • April 12, 1945 - January 20, 1953

BIRTHDATE: May 8, 1884
BIRTHPLACE: Lamar, Missouri
PHYSICAL DESCRIPTION: 5 ft. 9 in., 185 lbs.
EDUCATION: Kansas City Law School
RELIGION: Baptist
FIRST LADY: Elizabeth Wallace (Bess) Truman
CHILDREN: Margaret
MILITARY SERVICE: During World War I, he served with the 129th Field Artillery, rising from lieutenant to major.
POLITICAL PARTY: Democratic
VICE PRESIDENT: Alben W. Barkley
SALARY: First term - $75,000/year
          Second term - $100,000/year
NICKNAME: Man from Independence
DIED: December 26, 1972, in Kansas City, Missouri
BURIED: Harry S Truman Presidential Library and Museum, Independence, Missouri

ACCOMPLISHMENTS AND EVENTS

★ Oversaw conclusion of World War II; demanded unconditional surrender of Japan, ordered use of the atomic bomb on Hiroshima and Nagasaki.

★ Led the United States in helping create the United Nations.

★ Recognized the state of Israel.

★ To stop the spread of communism, created the Truman Doctrine and approved creation of the North Atlantic Treaty Organization.

★ Won U. N. mandate to expel the North Koreans from South Korea.

★ Taft-Hartley Act was passed, sustaining a worker's right not to join a union.

★ Established a Fair Employment Board to end racial discrimination in federal contracts.

★ Ordered that all armed services be racially integrated.

★ Increased minimum wage and extended Social Security coverage.

★ CONSTITUTIONAL AMENDMENT RATIFIED: 22nd Amendment, limiting presidents to two terms.

★ BEFORE THE PRESIDENCY: Bank clerk; Farmer; Haberdasher; Presiding Judge of Jackson County, Missouri; Member, U.S. Senate; Vice President of the United States

INTERESTING FACTS AND QUOTES

✦ He had a middle initial but no middle name.

✦ Enjoyed playing the piano; played the "Missouri Waltz" for guests.

✦ Bess Truman helped her husband write his speeches and make policy decisions but shunned the limelight. Known as her husband's "full partner," she died at the age of 97.

✦ DEWEY DEFEATS TRUMAN, newspaper headline prematurely announcing Truman's defeat in his bid for president.

✦ Feuded with music critics over his daughter's performances.

✦ "The buck stops here."

✦ "If you don't like the heat, get out of the kitchen."

✦ ASSASSINATION ATTEMPT: Survived an attack on the presidential residence by Puerto Rican nationalists. Twenty-three shots fired; president and family unharmed.

Dwight David Eisenhower

34th President • January 20, 1953 - January 20, 1961

BIRTHDATE: October 14, 1890
BIRTHPLACE: Denison, Texas
PHYSICAL DESCRIPTION: 5 ft. 10 in., 178 lbs.
EDUCATION: U.S. Military Academy at West Point; Command and General Staff School
RELIGION: Presbyterian
FIRST LADY: Marie Doud (Mamie) Eisenhower
CHILDREN: Dwight Doud, John Sheldon Doud
MILITARY SERVICE: Career military, rising to five-star general
POLITICAL PARTY: Republican
VICE PRESIDENT: Richard M. Nixon
SALARY: $100,000/year
NICKNAME: Ike
DIED: March 28, 1969, in Washington, D.C.
BURIED: Dwight D. Eisenhower Library and Museum, Abilene, Kansas

ACCOMPLISHMENTS AND EVENTS

★ Oversaw conclusion of Korean War.

★ Enunciated doctrine of United States' right to aid any country threatened by Communist aggression or subversion; established the Southeast Asia Treaty Organization.

★ Signed Civil Rights Act of 1960.

★ Enforced orders by U.S. Supreme Court for the integration of public schools, using federal troops when necessary. Made public facilities in Washington, D.C. available to people of all races.

★ Signed the bill authorizing construction of a 42,000-mile interstate highway system.

★ Created the Department of Health, Education and Welfare and the National Aeronautics and Space Administration (NASA).

★ "Hidden Hand" presidency used to describe his effectiveness as a leader behind the scenes.

★ ADMITTED TO THE UNION: Alaska, Hawaii

★ BEFORE THE PRESIDENCY: Supreme Allied Commander; Five Star General; President of Columbia University; Supreme Commander of the North Atlantic Treaty Organization

INTERESTING FACTS AND QUOTES

✦ He shot a hole-in-one on the golf course.

✦ He was the first president to have his pilot's license.

✦ He named the presidential retreat "Camp David" after his grandson.

✦ Richard Nixon's daughter, Julie, married President Eisenhower's grandson, David.

✦ Believed that those who serve in public office should promote and defend the public good, not special interests.

✦ He signed a bill to include the words "Under God" in the Pledge of Allegiance to the flag.

✦ As president, he instituted the interdenominational White House Prayer Breakfast and the practice of opening cabinet meetings with prayer.

"*A people that values its privileges above its principles soon loses both.*"

"*The only way to win World War III is to prevent it.*"

"And so, my fellow Americans: Ask not what your country can do for you—ask what you can do for your country."

John Fitzgerald Kennedy

35th President • January 20, 1961 - November 22, 1963

BIRTHDATE: May 29, 1917
BIRTHPLACE: Brookline, Massachusetts
PHYSICAL DESCRIPTION: 6 ft. 1/2 in., 170 lbs.
EDUCATION: Harvard University
RELIGION: Roman Catholic
FIRST LADY: Jacqueline Bouvier Kennedy
CHILDREN: Caroline, John, Jr., Patrick
MILITARY SERVICE: Served in the U.S. Navy during World War II, rising from ensign to lieutenant
POLITICAL PARTY: Democratic
VICE PRESIDENT: Lyndon B. Johnson
SALARY: $100,000/year
NICKNAME: JFK
DIED (IN OFFICE): November 22, 1963, in Dallas, Texas
BURIED: Arlington National Cemetery, Arlington, Virginia

ACCOMPLISHMENTS AND EVENTS

★ Cuban exiles, armed by the CIA, invaded Cuba; 1,100 survivors surrendered.

★ Established the Peace Corps, sending young Americans to developing countries to do humanitarian work.

★ Ordered end to discrimination in housing subsidized by federal funds; established the President's Committee on Equal Employment Opportunity.

★ Soviets built the Berlin Wall.

★ Negotiated Nuclear Test Ban Treaty banning nuclear testing in the atmosphere.

★ Space Program expanded; committed to placing an American on the moon during the decade.

★ Dr. Martin Luther King, Jr. delivered his "I Have a Dream" speech.

★ CONSTITUTIONAL AMENDMENT RATIFIED: 23rd Amendment, granting residents of the District of Columbia the right to vote in presidential elections.

★ ASSASSINATION: On November 22, 1963, Kennedy was shot while traveling in a motorcade in Dallas, Texas. Served 1,036 days in office.

★ BEFORE THE PRESIDENCY: Journalist; Member, U.S. House of Representatives; Member, U.S. Senate

INTERESTING FACTS AND QUOTES

✦ He was the first Roman Catholic president.

✦ Earned a Purple Heart and the Navy and Marine Corps Medal for rescuing members of his crew from the PT-109.

✦ His presidency defined the hopes and aspirations of a generation.

✦ First president born in the 20th century; the youngest president to be elected.

✦ Wrote *Profiles in Courage*, which won a Pulitzer Prize; the only president to win that prize.

✦ Engaged in first televised presidential debate.

✦ When hosting all of the Nobel Prize winners, he proclaimed, "I think this is the most extraordinary collection of intellectual talent ever gathered at the White House, with the possible exception of when Thomas Jefferson dined alone."

Lyndon Baines Johnson

36th President • November 22, 1963 - January 20, 1969

BIRTHDATE: August 27, 1908
BIRTHPLACE: near Stonewall, Texas
PHYSICAL DESCRIPTION: 6 ft. 3 in., 210 lbs.
EDUCATION: Southwest Texas State University; Georgetown Law School
RELIGION: Disciples of Christ
FIRST LADY: Claudia Taylor (Lady Bird) Johnson
CHILDREN: Lynda Bird, Luci Baines
MILITARY SERVICE: Lieutenant commander in the U.S. Navy during World War II
POLITICAL PARTY: Democratic
VICE PRESIDENT: Hubert H. Humphrey
SALARY: $100,000/year
NICKNAME: LBJ
DIED: January 22, 1973, at his ranch near Johnson City, Texas
BURIED: LBJ Ranch, near Johnson City, Texas

ACCOMPLISHMENTS AND EVENTS

★ Signed into law a number of anti-poverty measures including Job Corps, VISTA, Work-Study Program, Community Action Program, Head Start, Upward Bound, legal aid.

★ Signed Civil Rights legislation barring discrimination in employment, hotels, restaurants, public facilities, and housing, and outlawing discriminatory literacy tests.

★ Established Medicare and Medicaid, providing low cost medical insurance for the elderly and medical insurance for the poor.

★ Signed Water Quality Act and the Clean Water Restoration Act.

★ Signed Fair Packaging and Labeling Act and the Wholesome Meat Act.

★ Oversaw the escalation of the Vietnam War.

★ Dr. Martin Luther King, Jr. and Robert F. Kennedy were assassinated.

★ CONSTITUTIONAL AMENDMENTS RATIFIED: 24th Amendment, outlawing the poll tax, and the 25th Amendment, providing for filling a vacancy in the vice presidency.

★ BEFORE THE PRESIDENCY: Teacher; Director, National Youth Administration in Texas; Member, U.S. House of Representatives; Member, U.S. Senate; Vice President of the United States

INTERESTING FACTS AND QUOTES

✦ Following the assassination of President Kennedy, he was administered the presidential oath aboard Air Force One.

✦ First president sworn in by a woman.

✦ First president to circumnavigate the globe.

✦ First president to appoint an African-American cabinet member and an African-American to the Supreme Court.

✦ **As president, he worshipped at churches of various denominations; he was the first incumbent president to meet a pope.**

✦ "A president's hardest task is not to do what is right, but to know what is right."

"I've learned that only two things are necessary to keep one's wife happy. First, let her think she's having her own way. And second, let her have it."

"When Mr. Khrushchev says our grandchildren will live under Communism, let us say his grandchildren will live in freedom."

"Only if you have been in the deepest valley can you ever know how magnificent it is to be on the highest mountain."

76

Richard Milhous Nixon

37th President • January 20, 1969 - August 9, 1974

BIRTHDATE: January 9, 1913
BIRTHPLACE: Yorba Linda, California
PHYSICAL DESCRIPTION: 5 ft. 11 1/2 in., 175 lbs.
EDUCATION: Whittier College; Duke University Law School
RELIGION: Quaker
FIRST LADY: Thelma Ryan (Pat) Nixon
CHILDREN: Patricia, Julie
MILITARY SERVICE: Served as an officer in the U.S. Navy during World War II
POLITICAL PARTY: Republican
VICE PRESIDENT: First term - Spiro Agnew
Second term - Spiro Agnew, Gerald Ford
SALARY: $200,000/year
NICKNAME: Tricky Dick
DIED: April 22, 1994, in New York, New York
BURIED: Richard Nixon Library and Birthplace, Yorba Linda, California

ACCOMPLISHMENTS AND EVENTS

★ First U.S. president to visit China, opening the door for China's participation in world trade. Supported China's admission to the United Nations.

★ Expanded fighting into Cambodia and Laos, while reducing U.S. involvement in the Vietnam War by training South Vietnamese forces. Ended U.S. involvement in Vietnam.

★ Visited the Soviet Union and signed the Chemical Weapons Treaty (1971) with that country, in which both nations agreed to destroy their biological and chemical weapons stockpiles and to ban their further development.

★ Appointed Gerald Ford as Vice President when Spiro Agnew resigned; first use of the 25th Amendment provisions.

★ Created the Environmental Protection Agency (EPA) and signed the Clean Air Act of 1970.

★ Promoted the Indian Self-Determination and Education Assistance Act.

★ On July 20, 1969, Astronaut Neil Armstrong became the first man to set foot on the moon.

★ CONSTITUTIONAL AMENDMENT RATIFIED: 26th Amendment, lowering the voting age from 21 to 18; ratified in the shortest amount of time of all Constitutional amendments.

★ ASSASSINATION: On February 22, 1974, Samuel Byck hijacked an airliner with the intention of crashing it into the White House. In this foiled assassination attempt, the co-pilot and an airport security guard were killed by Byck.

INTERESTING FACTS AND QUOTES

✦ Had workers fill in the White House swimming pool with concrete to provide more space for the press.

✦ First president to resign the office; he resigned on August 9, 1974, to avoid inevitable impeachment because of the Watergate scandal.

✦ First president to voluntarily give up lifetime Secret Service protection.

✦ His headstone reminds onlookers that "the greatest honor history can bestow is the title of peacemaker."

✦ BEFORE THE PRESIDENCY: Lawyer; Member, U.S. House of Representatives; Member, U.S. Senate; Vice President of the United States

Gerald Rudolph Ford

38th President • August 9, 1974 - January 20, 1977

BIRTHDATE: July 14, 1913
BIRTHPLACE: Omaha, Nebraska
PHYSICAL DESCRIPTION: 6 ft., 195 lbs.
EDUCATION: University of Michigan; Yale Law School
RELIGION: Episcopalian
FIRST LADY: Elizabeth Warren (Betty) Ford
CHILDREN: Michael, John, Steven, Susan
MILITARY SERVICE: Served in the U.S. Navy from April 1942 to February 1946, rising from ensign to lieutenant commander
POLITICAL PARTY: Republican
VICE PRESIDENT: Nelson A. Rockefeller
SALARY: $200,000/year
NICKNAME: Jerry; Mr. Nice Guy

ACCOMPLISHMENTS AND EVENTS

★ Granted "a full, free and absolute pardon" to former President Nixon.

★ Offered clemency to thousands of Vietnam War Era draft evaders.

★ Communist victory in southeast Asia; Communists captured the capital of Saigon in Vietnam.

★ Signed legislation for $2.3 billion in short-term loans to New York City.

★ Created the Energy Research and Development Administration.

★ Signed Campaign Reform Law, providing public funding of presidential campaigns and strict limits on individual contributions.

★ Signed law extending the Voting Rights Act to include benefits for Spanish-speaking and other language minorities.

★ Signed into law the Indian Self-Determination and Education Assistance Act of 1975.

★ ASSASSINATION ATTEMPTS: Ford was the only president to face two assassination attempts; they occurred within 17 days of each other.

★ BEFORE THE PRESIDENCY: Lawyer; Member, U.S. House of Representatives; House Minority Leader; Vice President of the United States

INTERESTING FACTS AND QUOTES

✦ Turned down offers to play professional football from the Green Bay Packers and the Detroit Lions.

✦ Served as vice president and president and was not elected to either office. He became vice president upon the resignation of Spiro Agnew and became president upon the resignation of Richard Nixon.

✦ First Lady Betty Ford was known for outspoken support of women's rights.

✦ First president to issue a presidential pardon to a former president.

✦ "We are bound together by the most powerful of all ties, our fervent love for freedom and independence, which knows no homeland by the human heart."

"Our Constitution works. Our great Republic is a government of laws and not of men. Have the people rule."

79

"*The experience of democracy is like the experience of life itself-always changing, infinite in its variety...and all the more valuable for having been tested by adversity.*"

James Earl Carter, Jr.

39th President • January 20, 1977 - January 20, 1981

BIRTHDATE: October 1, 1924
BIRTHPLACE: Plains, Georgia
PHYSICAL DESCRIPTION: 5 ft. 9 1/2 in., 155 lbs.
EDUCATION: United States Naval Academy
RELIGION: Baptist
FIRST LADY: Rosalynn Smith Carter
CHILDREN: John, James Earl III, Jeffrey, Amy
MILITARY SERVICE: Served in the U.S. Navy from 1946 to 1953, rising from ensign to lieutenant
POLITICAL PARTY: Democratic
VICE PRESIDENT: Walter F. Mondale
SALARY: $200,000/year
NICKNAME: Jimmy

ACCOMPLISHMENTS AND EVENTS

★ On first day as president, pardoned 10,000 draft evaders of the Vietnam War era.

★ Signed legislation deregulating airlines, natural gas, and trucking.

★ Created the Department of Energy. Signed numerous environmental protection laws, as well as set aside 104 million acres in national parks, wildlife refuges, and wilderness areas.

★ Proclaimed human rights as a major foreign policy objective, condemning racism in South Africa and the regimes of Castro and Idi Amin. Won Nobel Peace Prize and devotes post-presidential life to humanitarian work.

★ Relinquished the Canal Zone to Panama.

★ Led intense negotiations with Egypt's Anwar Sadat and Israel's Menachem Begin, leading to the "Camp David Accords"; resulted in a peace treaty between Egypt and Israel.

★ Americans held hostage by Iran; 52 were held for 444 days.

★ BEFORE THE PRESIDENCY: Peanut farmer; Member, Georgia State Senate; Governor of Georgia

INTERESTING FACTS AND QUOTES

✦ First president to be born in a hospital.

✦ Separating himself from the "Imperial Presidency" established by Nixon, he and his family walked to the White House after the inauguration and sold the presidential yacht.

✦ First Lady Rosalynn Carter was known for her southern hospitality.

✦ He was one of three presidents who won the Nobel Peace Prize.

✦ "The passage of the civil rights acts during the 1960s was the greatest thing to happen to the South in my lifetime. It lifted a burden from the whites as well as the blacks."

✦ After the presidency, engaged in extensive diplomatic and humanitarian work.

Ronald Wilson Reagan

40th President • January 20, 1981 - January 20, 1989

BIRTHDATE: February 6, 1911
BIRTHPLACE: Tampico, Illinois
PHYSICAL DESCRIPTION: 6 ft. 1 in., 185 lbs.
EDUCATION: Eureka College
RELIGION: Disciples of Christ
FIRST LADY: Nancy Davis Reagan
CHILDREN: Maureen, Michael, Patricia, Ronald
MILITARY SERVICE: Army captain during World War II
POLITICAL PARTY: Republican
VICE PRESIDENT: George H. W. Bush
SALARY: $200,000/year
NICKNAME: Dutch; Great Communicator
DIED: June 5, 2004, in Los Angeles, California
BURIED: Reagan Presidential Library, Simi Valley, California

ACCOMPLISHMENTS AND EVENTS

★ Used "Reagonomics" in his economic policy: major tax cuts, deregulation, "trickle-down benefits." Net result was economic turnaround with massive national deficits.

★ Signed U.S.-Canadian Trade Pact, establishing free trade, abolishing tariffs on goods and services.

★ Nominated the first woman, Sandra Day O'Connor, to serve on the U.S. Supreme Court.

★ Tried to create a missile defense system called "Star Wars."

★ Accused of selling arms to Iran in exchange for the release of American hostages. Charges were filed against Oliver North and John Poindexter.

★ U.S. forces invaded the island of Grenada to rescue hundreds of Americans under threat from a leftist military coup.

★ Signed a treaty with the U.S.S.R. to limit nuclear weapons.

★ He opposed the proposed Equal Rights Amendment; ratification failed.

★ BEFORE THE PRESIDENCY: Actor; Governor of California

INTERESTING FACTS AND QUOTES

✦ The oldest president when elected, he was the first to have been divorced.

✦ Only professional actor to become president. He appeared in over 50 films.

✦ Served as president of the Screen Actors' Guild.

✦ While serving in the military, he appeared in Irving Berlin's musical film *This Is the Army* (1943).

✦ "What I'd really like to do is go down in history as the president who made Americans believe in themselves again."

✦ "Mr. Gorbachev, tear down this wall!"

✦ "Freedom is not the sole prerogative of a chosen few; it is the universal right of all God's children."

✦ ASSASSINATION ATTEMPT: President Reagan was shot in the chest by John Hinckley, Jr. at a Washington hotel two months after taking office.

"And let me add, to the party of Lincoln, there is no room for intolerance and not even a small corner for anti-Semitism of any kind. Many people are welcome in our house, but not the bigots."

"The surest way to win the war against poverty is to win the battle against ignorance. Even though we spend more on education than any other nation on Earth, we just don't measure up."

84

George Herbert Walker Bush

41st President • January 20, 1989 - January 20, 1993

BIRTHDATE: June 12, 1924
BIRTHPLACE: Milton, Massachusetts
PHYSICAL DESCRIPTION: 6 ft. 2 in., 195 lbs.
EDUCATION: Yale University
RELIGION: Episcopalian
FIRST LADY: Barbara Pierce Bush
CHILDREN: George, Robin, John, Neil, Marvin, Dorothy
MILITARY SERVICE: Served in the U.S. Navy in World War II
POLITICAL PARTY: Republican
VICE PRESIDENT: James Danforth Quayle
SALARY: $200,000/year
NICKNAME: Poppy

ACCOMPLISHMENTS AND EVENTS

★ Signed into law a plan to bail out hundreds of failed savings and loans.

★ Ordered invasion of Panama and the capture of General Manuel Noriega, who surrendered after 4 days of fighting.

★ Imposed economic sanctions on Iraq after its invasion of Kuwait, but the sanctions did not work. Launched Operation Desert Storm to defeat Iraq's army.

★ Communism collapsed and the Berlin Wall was torn down. Nations of Eastern Europe dismantled their Communist governments.

★ Signed Americans with Disabilities Act, landmark legislation requiring places of business and public accommodations to make their facilities accessible to those in wheelchairs.

★ Signed Clean Air Act of 1990, strengthening anti-pollution standards, reducing acid rain, urban smog and toxic chemicals emissions.

★ Established the Points of Light Foundation, encouraging Americans to volunteer in their communities.

★ CONSTITUTIONAL AMENDMENT RATIFIED: 27th Amendment, providing that changes in congressional compensation cannot take effect until after the following congressional election. Originally submitted in 1789, this ratification took the longest time in U.S. history.

INTERESTING FACTS AND QUOTES

✦ Became youngest pilot then in the U.S. Navy in 1943. Flew 58 combat missions. Awarded the Distinguished Flying Cross for completing the mission in spite of attack on his airplane by the enemy.

✦ Assigned to the Oceana Naval Air Station in Virginia in 1944.

✦ Second president to be father of a president.

✦ First sitting vice president to be elected president since Martin Van Buren in 1836.

✦ One of three presidents to have a pilot's license.

✦ Only president to parachute out of an airplane, including once on his 75th birthday and again on his 80th birthday.

✦ BEFORE THE PRESIDENCY: Equipment salesman; President/CEO of oil drilling company; Member, U.S. House of Representatives; U.S. Ambassador to the United Nations; Chairman of Republican National Committee; Chief U.S. Liaison in China; Director of the Central Intelligence Agency; Vice President of the United States

William Jefferson Clinton

42nd President • January 20, 1993 - January 20, 2001

BIRTHDATE: August 19, 1946
BIRTHPLACE: Hope, Arkansas
PHYSICAL DESCRIPTION: 6 ft. 2 in., 220 lbs.
EDUCATION: Georgetown University; Oxford University; Yale Law School
RELIGION: Southern Baptist
FIRST LADY: Hillary Rodham Clinton
CHILDREN: Chelsea
MILITARY SERVICE: None
POLITICAL PARTY: Democratic
VICE PRESIDENT: Albert A. Gore, Jr.
SALARY: $200,000/year
NICKNAME: Bubba, the Comeback Kid, Slick Willie

ACCOMPLISHMENTS AND EVENTS

★ Productivity rose, unemployment fell, and the stock market reached unprecedented heights. Clinton was able to balance the Federal budget and produce an unparalleled budget surplus.

★ Promising to have a Cabinet that "looks like America," he is noted for the appointment of women and people from minority groups to the Cabinet and other high government positions.

★ Israeli Prime Minister Rabin and PLO leader Arafat signed the Declaration of Principles, granting Palestinians self-rule on the West Bank and Gaza; first signed agreement between Jews and Palestinians.

★ Signed the Brady Handgun Violence Prevention Act requiring a background check and a waiting time to buy handguns.

★ The Alfred R. Murrah Federal Building in Oklahoma City was bombed on April 19, 1995, killing 168 people.

★ Signed bills to reform the welfare system, increase the minimum wage, and reduce taxes.

★ Signed the Family and Medical Leave Act, allowing parents who are caring for family members or newborns to keep their jobs.

★ In the second presidential Constitutional confrontation with the Congress, Clinton was impeached by the House of Representatives and tried, but not convicted, by the Senate.

★ Sent U.S. troops to Bosnia as part of a NATO peacekeeping force to stop ethnic cleansing activities of Serbian troops and government.

INTERESTING FACTS AND QUOTES

✦ At the age of 32, he was the youngest governor in the country.

✦ Our first president to have been a Rhodes Scholar.

✦ First president to play a saxophone.

✦ First president to use the line-item veto.

✦ Hillary Clinton was the only First Lady to assume public office; she was elected U.S. Senator from New York upon leaving the White House.

✦ "We must teach our children to resolve their conflicts with words, not weapons."

✦ "There is nothing wrong with America that cannot be cured with what is right with America."

✦ BEFORE THE PRESIDENCY: Law professor; Attorney General of Arkansas; Governor of Arkansas

"If you live long enough, you'll make mistakes. But if you learn from them, you'll be a better person. It's how you handle adversity, not how it affects you. The main thing is never quit, never quit, never quit."

"Our Nation - this generation - will lift a dark threat of violence from our people and our future. We will rally the world to this cause by our efforts, by our courage. We will not tire, we will not falter, we will not fail."

George Walker Bush

43rd President • January 20, 2001 -

BIRTHDATE: July 6, 1946
BIRTHPLACE: New Haven, Connecticut
PHYSICAL DESCRIPTION: 5 ft. 11 in., 190 lbs.
EDUCATION: Yale University; Harvard Business School
RELIGION: Methodist
FIRST LADY: Laura Welch Bush
CHILDREN: Jenna, Barbara
MILITARY SERVICE: F-102 fighter pilot in the Texas Air National Guard
POLITICAL PARTY: Republican
VICE PRESIDENT: Richard B. Cheney
SALARY: $400,000/year
NICKNAME: Dubya

ACCOMPLISHMENTS AND EVENTS

★ Established the White House Office of Faith-Based and Community Initiatives to support churches that provide social services to those in need.

★ No Child Left Behind legislation signed into law.

★ Championed and signed a multi-billion dollar plan to give prescription drug coverage to Medicare recipients.

★ Signed a $1.35 trillion tax cut bill providing immediate refunds to all taxpayers and lowering tax rates over a 10-year period.

★ September 11, 2001: Al-Qaeda terrorists attacked the United States by hijacking four passenger airliners and crashing them into the World Trade Center, the Pentagon, and a field in Pennsylvania, killing thousands of innocent people.

★ Enlisted millions of Americans in volunteer service through the USA Freedom Corps in the aftermath of 9/11/01.

★ In the aftermath of terrorist attacks, the USA Patriot Act is passed, granting the executive branch vastly expanded investigatory and enforcement powers.

★ Created the Department of Homeland Security, the largest federal agency in U.S. history, to protect the nation from foreign attacks.

★ Ordered a full-scale military invasion of Iraq, resulting in the overthrow of the Iraqi regime and the capture of President Saddam Hussein.

INTERESTING FACTS AND QUOTES

✦ Son of our 41st president, he is the first son of a president to become president since John Quincy Adams.

✦ **Laura Bush, an advocate for children and education, received a master's degree in library science and worked as a teacher and librarian before her marriage.**

✦ One of three presidents to have his pilot's license.

✦ First president to have fathered twins.

✦ His election marked the first time that the U.S. Supreme Court was involved in a presidential election, raising Constitutional issues.

✦ "In our grief and anger, we have found our mission and our moment."

✦ BEFORE THE PRESIDENCY: Oil businessman; Baseball team owner; Governor of Texas

1. This president could write both Greek and Latin with either hand at the same time.

2. This president was the only president elected by a unanimous vote. He could have been king.

3. This president said, "That if you expect a people to be ignorant and free, then you expect something that never was nor never will be."

4. These two presidents, who were once political adversaries, became close friends. They both died on July 4th, 1826, 50 years to the day after the adoption of the Declaration of Independence.

5. This was our only president to have been a prisoner of war. When he was inaugurated, he had a saber slash down his forehead and two bullets in his body. The one closest to his heart came from fighting a duel; the other one was removed from his shoulder after he took office.

6. This president made the longest inaugural speech and served the shortest term.

7. These two presidents are our only two from the same county in the same state and were elected as president and vice president at the same time and served as consecutive presidents.

8. This president was born in 1790 and his grandson is alive in 2004.

9. This president said, "It is better to remain silent and be thought a fool than to open one's mouth and remove all doubt."

10. This president did not allow liquor or spirits to be served in the White House. His wife became known as Lemonade Lucy. The press reported that after one state function, everybody had a gala time and the water flowed like wine. Lucy was the first First Lady with a college degree.

11. He was born in a log cabin. He was an indentured servant and ran away at the age of 15 (a reward was offered for his return). He never went to school. After he was married, his wife tutored him in how to read and write. He was a tailor and made his own clothes.

12. This president became president of Princeton University. He also won the Nobel Peace Prize. He was the only president to earn his Ph.D.

13. This president was elected to office two non-consecutive terms. Thus he became our 22nd and our 24th president. He was the only president to be married in the White House. The words "love, honor and keep" were substituted for "love, honor and obey". His wedding was performed at 7:00 p.m. in the blue room of the White House so that he could work on his wedding day. She was 21 and he was 49. As a young man, he worked as a clerk in a store for $50.00 a year plus room and board.

14. This president was very quiet and shy. When a lady at a dinner party informed him that she had made a wager that she could make him say more than two words, his reply was, "You lose." One of his critics was informed of his passing and asked the question, "how can you tell?"

15. This president served as vice-president and then president and was not elected to either office.

16. This president had offers to play professional football from the Green Bay Packers and the Detroit Lions.

17. This president appeared in over 50 films.

18. This president was a peanut farmer and the first president to ride underwater in a nuclear submarine.

19. This president said "Don't ask what your country can do for you, ask what you can do for your country."

20. When hosting all of the Nobel prize winners, he proclaimed, "I think this is the most extraordinary collections of intellectual talent ever gathered at the White House, with the possible exception of when Thomas Jefferson dined alone."

21. These two men became the first father and son to be elected president.

22. This president was the grandson of another president.

23. This was our only president to have been a Rhodes scholar and his wife became a United States senator.

24. These two presidents were another father/son, one being 41st and the other the 43rd.

25. This president had a middle initial but not a middle name.

26. When an opponent called him two-faced, his response was, "if I had two faces, do you think I would be wearing this one."

27. He was the only president to receive a patent. This patent was for lifting vessels over shoals by inflating air chambers near the water line.

ANSWERS

1. James A. Garfield; 2. George Washington; 3. Thomas Jefferson; 4. Thomas Jefferson and John Adams; 5. Andrew Jackson; 6. William H. Harrison; 7. William H. Harrison and John Tyler; 8. John Tyler; 9. Abraham Lincoln; 10. Rutherford B. Hayes; 11. Andrew Johnson; 12. Woodrow Wilson; 13. Grover Cleveland; 14. Calvin Coolidge 15. Gerald Ford; 16. Gerald Ford; 17. Ronald Reagan; 18. James Carter; 19. John F. Kennedy; 20. John F. Kennedy; 21. John Adams and John Quincy Adams; 22. Benjamin Harrison; 23. William Clinton; 24. George Bush and George W. Bush; 25. Harry S Truman; 26. Abraham Lincoln; 27. Abraham Lincoln

Bibliography and Resources

Boller, Paul F., Jr. *Presidential Wives, An Anecdotal History. Revised Edition.* New York: Oxford University Press, 1998.

Bowman, John. *The History of the American Presidency.* JG Press, North Dighton, MA: World Publications Group, Inc., 2002.

Degregorio, William A. *The Complete Book of U.S. Presidents.* New York: Barricade Books, 1996.

Dole, Bob. *Great Presidential Wit (... I Wish I Was in the Book).* New York: Simon & Schuster, 2001.

Ellis, Joseph J. *Founding Brothers.* New York: Alfred A. Kroft, 2001.

Frank, Sid and Melick, Arden Davis. *The Presidents Tidbits & Trivia.* New York: Crown Publishers, Inc., 1984.

Garrison, Webb. *A Treasury of White House Tales.* Nashville: Rutledge Hill Press, 1989.

Hunt, Trevor, ed., *Words from our Presidents; Quips and Quotes from George Washington to George W. Bush.* New York: Gramercy Books, 2001.

Kane, Joseph Nathan, Podell, Janet, and Anzovin, Steven. *Facts About the Presidents.* New York: The H.W. Wilson Company, 2001.

Kochmann, Rachel M. *Presidents Birthplaces, Homes, and Burial Sites.* Osage, MN: Osage Publicatons, 2002.

Kunhardt, Philip B. Jr., Kunhartdt, Philip B. III, and Kunhardt, Peter W. *The American President.* New York: Riverhead Books, 1999.

Jacobson, Doranne. *Presidents & First Ladies of the United States.* New York: Todtri Book Publishers, 1995.

Lamb, Brian and the C-SPAN staff. *Who's Buried in Grant's Tomb?* Washington, D.C.: National Cable Satellite Corporation, 2000.

Marton, Kati. *Hidden Power: Presidential Marriages that Shaped our History.* New York: Random House, 2001.

McCullough, David. *John Adams.* New York: Simon & Schuster, 2001.

McPherson, James M., ed., *"To the Best of My Ability": The American Presidents.* An Agincourt Press Publication, Society of American Historians. New York: Dorling Kindersley, 2000.

Rubel, David. *The Scholastic Encyclopedia of the Presidents and Their Times.* New York: Scholastic, Inc., 1994.

Saunders, Robert M. *Power, the Presidency, and the Preamble: Interpretative Essays on Selected Presidents of the United States.* Westport, CT: Praeger Press, 2002.

Internet Sources

The White House government website: www.whitehouse.gov

Library of Congress website: www.thomas.gov

Miller Center for Public Affairs at the University of Virginia: www.americanpresident.org

C-SPAN's website companion to the American Presidents series: www.americanpresidents.org

Jefferson's year-round retreat website: www.poplarforest.org

Website of the home of President Andrew Jackson: www.thehermitage.com

University of Michigan's internet public library: www.ipl.org

The President Richard M. Nixon library: www.nixonfoundation.org

The Ashbrook Center for Public Affairs at Ashland University: www.ashbrook.org

The Grolier Encyclopedia online, the American Presidents: http://ap.grolier.com/

DAVID ADICKES

David Adickes, the internationally known artist who created the monumental sculptures at Presidents Park, has paintings and sculptures displayed in several major art museums across the country. His works include an 8-foot bronze statue of President George H.W. Bush located at Bush Intercontinental Airport in Houston, Texas. Famed author James A. Michener, in his book, *Adickes: A Portfolio With Critique*, commented that a sketch of him done by Adickes was "the best portrait ever done of me; it looks more like me than an accurate photograph".

STATUE FACTS

✦ The statues are made of cast Portland concrete over steel armatures.

✦ They were fabricated in Houston and transported to Virginia on flat-bed trucks and reassembled here.

✦ Properly maintained they should last hundreds of years.

✦ The statues weigh an average of 7,500 pounds each, having a combined weight of approximately 315,000 pounds.

✦ The statues stand 16 to 18 feet tall, having a combined height of approximately 700 feet.

✦ It took five years to produce 42 statues. Mr. Adickes started this 5-year project when he was 68 years old.

Selected Defining Moments
of American History

Five of Presidents Park's Defining Moments signs play music from the period of the defining moment time frame on a continuous basis. A push button overrides the music for a significant message as follows:

- *The American Revolution* depicts Patrick Henry's "Give Me Liberty or Give Me Death" speech at St. John's Church in Richmond, Colony of Virginia, on March 23, 1775.

- *The Civil War* depicts Abraham Lincoln's Gettysburg Address of November 19, 1863 in Gettysburg, PA.

- *Protecting Our National Resources* depicts Theodore Roosevelt's valiant efforts to further establish natural conservation in the American west with quotes from his 1905 publication entitled: "Outdoor Pastimes of An American Hunter."

- *The Civil Rights Movement* depicts Reverend Martin Luther King's "I Had A Dream" speech in Washington, DC on August 8, 1963.

- *The Newburgh Conspiracy* depicts General George Washington's letter to Colonial Lewis Nikolai dated May 22, 1782, as well as his farewell address to his officers at a church in Newburgh, New York on March 15, 1783.

In addition, there are nine other selected Defining Moments of American History featured throughout the park:

- *The Founding Documents*
- *Territorial Expansion*
- *Labor Movement*
- *World War I*
- *September 11, 2001*

- *Great Depression*
- *World War II*
- *Landing on the Moon*
- *Korea, Cold War & Superpower*

Each sign features a large display with a powerful message that is further illustrated in our "Defining Moments" book by noted historian and author James A. Crutchfield.

About Presidents Park

The Mission of Presidents Park is to promote a better understanding of the American presidency, foster an appreciation for our presidents as individuals, encourage civic responsibility and involvement, and provide educational opportunities of the highest standards.

Educational Programs offered by Presidents Park include admission to the park, a guided tour, and teacher materials. All educational programs are adaptable into elementary, middle and high school levels. All programs have been correlated to the Virginia Standards of Learning for Social Studies.

Guided Theme Tours and Themed Adult Packages offered by Presidents Park give a wide range of themed tours that are fun and enhance the educational experience of the park. Offerings of First Ladies Afternoon Tea and Evening Tour & Dessert Receptions give a great range of tour and tasty selections with the Presidents.

Presidents Park Café offers a variety of group menus including bag lunches and special themed meals prepared by Chef Rey Olivo. Chef Rey retired from the Air Force as a Command Chef and prepared food for then Vice-President George H.W. Bush and foreign dignitaries. He is the author of two Heart Healthy Cookbooks and was selected to train other military chefs including George Schwarzkopf's on healthy heart menus. Presidents Park is proud to have Chef Rey in charge of our food operations. The Café serves a variety of family menu items as well as meals saluting presidential tastes. Many of our themed meals are served in the private banquet room overlooking the garden and monuments of the park.

Presidents Park Gift Shop features a wide selection of presidential gift items, food, jewelry, apparel, educational books by renowned authors and souvenirs. Teacher resources and educational games are also available to enhance the learning experience. Gift Shop selections are available for purchase on our website: www.presidentspark.org.

The Museum is fully accessible for people using wheelchairs and motorized scooters. A few wheelchairs are available for use around the park and are free. Benches are conveniently located throughout the park. A garden gazebo is situated to provide shade and seating during your tour.

Facilities include a café, sundeck, veranda, observation balcony and private banquet room. Enjoy dining while overlooking America's 42 presidents.

Educational Tours

Presidents Park offers a variety of educational tours featuring events involving all of the United States presidents. These tours are designated to inspire, motivate and educate with a heightened sense of patriotism.

Five school group tours are offered in three separate grade levels. Each tour has been formulated by Presidents Park's Board of Education to meet the Virginia Standards of Learning.

Patriot Theme tours are tailored to groups of all ages from preschoolers to seniors. Patriot Theme tour contents have been reviewed by Presidents Park's National Council of Scholars for content accuracy.

For more information regarding Presidents Park's Educational Programs please contact Winette Jeffery, Presidents Park's Director of Education at wjeffery@presidentspark.org.